HOPKINSVILLE

HOPKINSVILLE

A Memoir in Prose Poems

T. Crunk

Accents Publishing • Lexington, Kentucky • 2025

Printed in the United States of America

Accents Publishing
Editor: Katerina Stoykova
Cover photo by Joann Crunk. Used by permission of the author.

Library of Congress Control Number: 2025937418
ISBN: 978-1-961127-15-9
First Edition

accents
publishing

Accents Publishing is an independent press for brilliant voices. For a catalog of current and upcoming titles, please visit us on the Web at

www.accents-publishing.com

CONTENTS

Hobo Signs / 1
Praying Hands / 5
Seining / 9
Kentucky Orphans Aid Society / 15
Elk Brand Mfg. Co. / 19
West Side / 23
World Book Encyclopedia / 27
Bethel Baptist Church / 29
Dry Branch / 35
Fire / 39

Night Light / 43
Downtown / 45
Illinois Central Freight Depot / 49
The Kentucky Club / 53
Wreck of the Titanic / 57

Bristol / 61
Twilight Speedway / 65
Brass Eagles / 71
The Blue Rose / 73

Christmas, Bainbridge Grove Missionary Baptist Church / 83
Glass Bottom Boats / 87
Evansville / 91
Nashville / 97
Fair Week / 103
The Alhambra / 109
Screaming Eagles / 111

Iron Bridge / 123
Tiny Town / 129
Benny / 137
Saturday Night / 143
Sunrise Service / 147
Sunday Morning / 151

Acknowledgments / 155

About the Author / 157

For Kate Youngs & Rev. Marvin Stinson

For Jo & Barney

For Irvine, Roy & Golda

For Luca

Hobo Signs

It was my mother's job to look for hobo signs.

They would be scratched on the wall of the shed or on one of the trash barrels or one of the fence slats, with chalk or charcoal or a knife. She even found them scratched into the crossties of the tracks running just behind the fence.

She didn't know what any of them meant. But she knew they told you whether you were welcome at a certain house, whether it was a good place to stop for food or clothes or work, or whether it was best not to stop. Her job was to rub them off or scratch over them, so you couldn't tell what they were.

Her father said he didn't mind helping a man out, but he wasn't running a tramp hotel, either. And since he was a preacher, they were likely to get more traffic than most anyway. If one did come to the door, they would try to give him something if they could, but there were many times they just didn't have anything to give.

My mother once watched her mother give a man the bowl of cornbread batter she was stirring up for supper, the only thing she had that she could part with. Her mother didn't like the looks of the man when he came to the door asking for something to eat, wouldn't let him in the house, so told him to come around to the kitchen window, where she handed the bowl and the wooden mixing spoon out to him.

The man sat under the shade tree in the yard and scooped the batter into his mouth, left the empty bowl and spoon in the grass and went on his way.

They would pass by most often in the late afternoon or early evening, headed for the camping place they had down the tracks a ways, beyond the cemetery at the edge of town. The camp was just a clearing in some scrub pine, where they could have a fire. They had put up a couple of lean-tos with some old sheet tin and lumber scraps and tar paper.

Sometimes people would take a box of old clothes or some food out and leave it for them.

★　　★　　★　　★

My mother always knew she was adopted, doesn't remember anybody telling her that much. And her mother reminded her of it often enough. They told her they had gotten her at an orphanage in Louisville.

She says that at some point she began to be afraid—afraid that if her mother and father had gotten her at an orphanage, then they could take her back any time they wanted, any time she did something that made them sorry they had gotten her.

And she would wonder, of course, where her real mother and father were. She figured that her mother must have died, because mothers don't just give their children away. But she thought her father might still be out there somewhere.

She started to wonder whether he might be one of them, if he might come walking down the tracks one evening and see her and stop for her.

He would tell her other mother and father that he had come to get her, to take her back home. She would go inside and gather up her belongings while he waited for her. She would come out and kiss her other mother and father, and tell them thank you. They would be crying. Then the two of them would set off together, disappearing down the tracks.

She started keeping all her important things—her Pinky and Blue Boy paper dolls, the painted thimbles her grandmother had given her, her Sunday hair clips—all together in a shoe box under her bed that she could just pick up and walk out with if she had to.

She started sitting on the back steps as late into the evening as she was let to, watching the tracks. She wondered if there was a hobo sign that meant, "Stop here. Your lost daughter lives here."

She wondered whether he would stop if he saw it scratched into one of the fence slats.

★ ★ ★ ★

One evening, my mother and a couple of her friends snuck down the tracks to the cemetery to spy on the hobo camp.

They hid in the trees and watched them—dark shadows shaped like men, sitting, leaning into their fire, holding their hands over it, hunched against the chill, their faces and their hands lit up.

They scared her, the look of them.

That night, and several nights afterwards, she lay awake as long as she could, not wanting to sleep, afraid that she would dream of them, stepping out of the darkness.

But, then, she began to think that if her real father were one of them, that is how he would come to her—out of the black trees and across the tracks toward her, his face lit yellow and flickering, his body of shadow, his shining hands reaching for her—

She knew that she would still go to him.

Praying Hands

Before they built the lake, it sat on a bluff overlooking the river, and they called it "The Castle on the Cumberland." And it looks like a castle, with high gray stone walls, towers at the corners, and a tall iron gate. Now, it juts out into the lake, surrounded on three sides by water, and they call it "The Kentucky Alcatraz."

My brother and I have been promised new billfolds, so we drive over one Sunday afternoon to get them. Across the highway from the big main gate is a stand, a little clapboard guard house, where they sell leather goods the convicts make.

There is only room enough inside for a couple of people at a time, so we have to wait outside until it's our turn. Just inside the open door, we can see a guard in a uniform sitting on a high stool. We see purses and moccasins and belts hanging from pegs along the walls, shelves stacked with billfolds and watchbands and coin purses. We can smell the leather, even outside the door.

While we're waiting, we go over and look at the lake. We read a sign that says, during the Civil War, the Confederates stretched a big chain across the river to try to stop the Union boats from getting through, but it didn't work.

When it's finally our turn to go in, the little room is stuffy and dark. When my eyes adjust, I see a high counter in the back of the room, with a kind of wire cage around it. A man in convict clothes is standing there.

My mother shows my father some of the purses. My brother and I look at billfolds. He picks a black one with praying hands carved into it. I pick a brown one with a German shepherd's head.

When we go to pay, my father puts the money on the counter and slides it through an opening in the wire cage. The man in convict clothes won't reach for it until my father's hands are off the counter. On our way out, my father nods to the guard. He nods back.

When we get to the car, my mother gives my brother and me a dollar apiece to put in our new billfolds.

Coming back that night, we stop for hamburgers. Then the long drive home.

I see lights in the houses across the fields and on the hillsides. I count fence posts or telephone poles. When my father tosses a cigarette butt out the window, I turn and watch it hit the road, watch the sparks fly up. It looks like little red and yellow fireworks going off.

Then I lay my head as far back as I can on the car seat, so I can look up through the rear window and see the stars spread out against the sky. I link them together, like connect-the-dots, making up my own constellations. I see—

a hammer

                             then a coal bucket

          a twelve

                a lock

                 a key

    angel's wing

                                    praying hands

Seining

You make a seine by splitting a burlap feed sack along the seams, stretching it out and wrapping each end around a bean pole. My grandfather shows us how, my brother and me, the three of us squatting on the creek bank in our old clothes. He tells us this is how he would fish for supper when he was a boy, and even a few times after he was grown, when he had to.

The early fog draws back off the water into the trees, leaving a film of mist on the car, which is pulled into the brush under a willow. The crickets and katydids are slow and quiet. They'll get louder as the morning warms up.

Once or twice a summer he takes us out like this, just the three of us, out in the country, so he can show us places. One year he took us over into Todd County to try to find the house he grew up in. Another year he took us up to Pine Bluff to try to find the cave he used to sleep in when he went out hunting.

Today, he's taking us seining.

It takes three people to fish with a seine. Two take the bean poles and stand them straight up in the water, with the feed sack stretched out between them. The third one holds the sack up in the middle so it won't droop down. Then you walk up the creek, holding it like that, so the sack is like a net, and when a fish swims toward you, the two on the ends try to close the bean poles around it, trapping it.

After we make our seine, we find a place where the bank flattens out, the grass growing down into the water, and we wade in. We start working our way upstream, through the sheltering trees.

My grandfather and brother work the poles, and I hold the net up in the middle. I watch the water striders drifting along the surface and the minnows flashing at my legs as we walk through them.

Working our way upstream, my grandfather tells us stories.

He tells about growing up with a father who was hardly ever home and drunk when he was; about being his mother's oldest child, the only boy, with three younger sisters; about his mother telling him when he was thirteen, that she just couldn't feed them all anymore, and that he would have to leave out on his own.

10

The year he took us to Todd County, we had to leave the car parked at a blind man's house and walk back through the woods a long while. We saw a red fox skitter past a caneberry thicket. We saw a possum's skull lying in a patch of wild asparagus.

When we got to my grandfather's house, it was nothing but part of the rock chimney rising up above the thistle and the goldenrod, some of the floorboards and a few foundation stones.

We walked around it, and my grandfather stooped down now and then to pick something up off the ground. But it would just be a rock or a bit of cinder, and he would pitch it off into the weeds.

Today, as we work our way up the creek, we scramble a few times, trying to catch something, and we almost get a couple of bluegill, but they're too fast for us.

We come to a gravel shallows and stop for a few minutes. My grandfather searches around until he finds some small white rocks that are round, but flattened off on two ends. He doesn't know what they are, but they're all over this part of the county. He says people used to call them mule's teeth.

We head on upstream, pass under an old iron bridge, and the water gets suddenly deep. He calls this the baptizing pool, and this is how he knew about this place. A mile or so downstream, the creek runs behind a church he used to pastor many years ago, and this is where they did the baptizings.

We climb out onto the bank and rest a while.

One year, he told us how, when he left home, he made his way out west and joined the threshing crews that followed the wheat harvest from Texas up through Iowa and the Dakotas and into Canada.

He liked working the animals, the mules and the horses, but he liked the big machines even more—the tractors and steam threshers, the boilers pumping, gear-works churning, the big belts slapping along the drive wheels. He said that if he hadn't been a preacher, he thinks he'd like to be a train engineer.

The year he took us to Pine Bluff, we stopped at a store to ask about the best way to get up to the caves. A couple of old men sitting around told us how, but said we'd better take our pistols because it was crawling with rattlesnakes up there. We decided not to try it, and drove over to Pilot Rock instead.

Pilot Rock is a giant stone hill, the tallest place in the county. There's a path around the back, then up, with some rickety wooden steps, so people can climb it.

When we got to the top, we could see everything for miles.

My grandfather showed us the monument at Jefferson Davis's birthplace in Fairview. You could just barely see it, but well enough to make out what it was. When my grandfather came back from out west, he worked on it a while, when they were building it.

Now after our rest, we wade back into the creek and work our way back downstream to where we started. By then the morning is getting on, the sun well above the trees, the crickets and katydids loud and sharp. We haven't caught anything, and I wonder if we really would have cooked it and eaten it if we had.

Instead, we eat the lunch my grandmother has made us—chicken, fried potato sandwiches, sweet pickles and boiled eggs, a thermos of coffee for my grandfather, two small bottles of coke for me and my brother.

We take our time eating, sitting out in the sun to let our clothes dry on us.

One time my grandfather told us about being called to be a preacher; of wrestling with the idea of it; of praying one night for the Lord to send him a sign if that's what He wanted him to do; of waking up the next morning and seeing a redbird perched on the bedroom windowsill, looking at him—all the sign he needed.

Later, I said, "Wonder why the Lord sent a redbird, instead of maybe a bluejay or a woodpecker?"

"Well, I never thought to ask," he said. "But I sure will one day."

When we're finished eating, we toss our chicken bones into the weeds, pack up our seine and start home.

We pull out of the underbrush and onto the gravel road. I sit in the back seat, behind my grandfather. He's whistling quietly, under his breath, the way he does when he doesn't want to talk. My brother's in the passenger seat, hanging his arm out the window, gliding his hand through the air.

My legs are tired. They feel like I'm still in the water, pushing upstream, against the current.

At the iron bridge, we slow down and ease across the clattering, thumping planks. I look down at the sunlight sparkling off the baptizing pool, the creek shallowing off beyond a gravel spit.

For the first time, I realize that, one day, I will remember this.

I look to where the creek disappears around a bend, beyond a willow cove, and start trying.

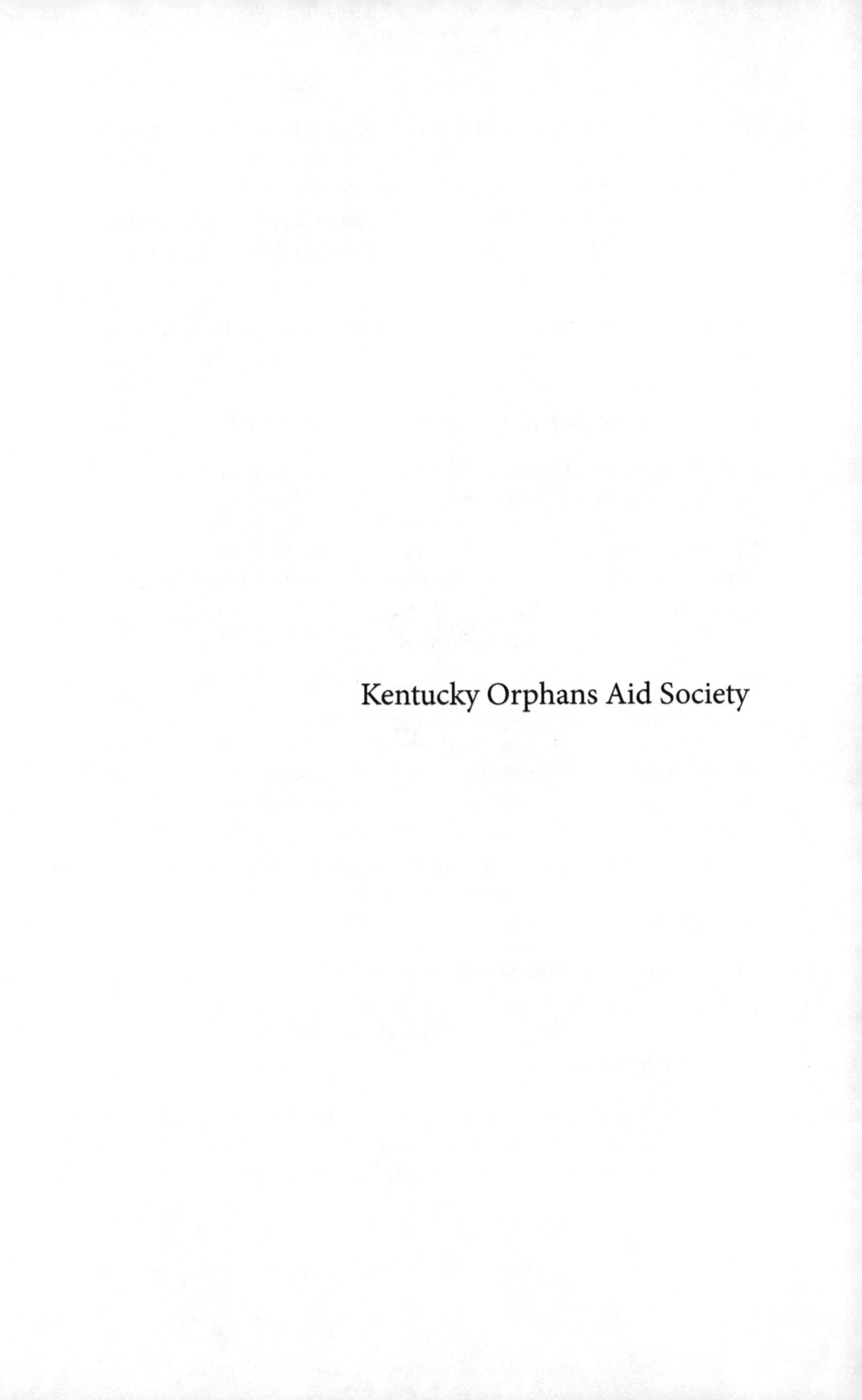

Kentucky Orphans Aid Society

My mother says she remembers being carried across an open field, a pasture maybe, or plowed ground, or a field of cornstubble. It was cold, and her head was wrapped up, so she couldn't see. But she was being carried by a boy, an older boy, and a second boy was following along behind, begging the first one to please not take her, begging him to be careful and not drop her.

Then, she remembers lying in a crib with another baby, in a small room crowded with other cribs. Hers was in the back of the room, beside a fireplace. She remembers a woman in a purple dress and a man with glasses walking through the room, stopping at the cribs.

When they came to her, she started crying. The woman reached down and picked her up. She was wearing a blue necklace.

Those are the two things my mother claims to remember. And every time she tells them, she says the same thing—she knows that people say you can't remember that far back, but she does. Even though both things must have happened before she was a year old.

★　　　★　　　★

She always knew she was adopted, but her mother had always told her they'd gotten her from an orphanage in Louisville. Her mother told how they first picked out a little boy to adopt, and took him back to the hotel with them for the trip home the next day, but during the night, her father decided he wished they'd gotten a little girl instead, so the next day they took the little boy back and got her. It was her father who wanted to go back for her.

And, in later years, the few times she ever asked about it, they told her the orphanage had burned down, and all the records were lost, so there was no way she could go back and find out anything about where she was born or who her family was.

Her Aunt Kitten finally told her the truth. She was left for adoption at the Willowdale Orphans Home in Bowling Green. It was the Depression, and like everybody else at the time, the orphanage was just scraping by, trying to feed what children they already had. Plus, more and more were getting left there, and fewer and fewer people were able to take them in.

So they started putting groups of children on trains and taking them around to different towns in that end of the state to try to find homes for them. They would go into a town and stay a week or so. Church people would put them up, help feed them. They would put announcements in the newspapers and church bulletins.

Her father was preaching at a church in Todd County at the time, and they came into Elkton and adopted my mother off the orphan train when it stopped there.

For a while, when my mother was growing up, her mother would tell her often that she ought to be grateful for what they had done for her by adopting her and providing for her, that if it wasn't for them, she might have done a whole lot worse. Then she said that to my mother one time after Aunt Kitten had told her the truth, and my mother said back that if it hadn't been for them she might have done a whole lot better too, and my grandmother slapped her for talking back to her, but didn't say that to my mother again.

★   ★   ★

I've only seen it once, though my mother has mentioned it many times over the years. She keeps it folded up in a little china box, tucked in a corner of her cedar chest. The box has a pink china rose on top, with one of the petals chipped off.

She brought it out that one time to show us.

The top of the paper says, "Kentucky Orphans Aid Society." In the upper left corner, stamped in red ink, is a picture of a little girl, her face upturned, her arms stretched up, reaching, with the caption, "Give A Child A Hand."

The bottom right corner of the paper is torn off. Above the tear is a space that says, "Adoptive Name," and it's inked in with the name I know my mother by. But below that is a space that says, "Given Name," and that's the part that's torn off.

My mother was five or six when she first saw it, found it hidden in the bottom of her mother's cedar chest. She could read well enough by then to tell what the paper was, but wasn't able to make out that much of it before she had to sneak it back in the chest.

She was, though, able to make out the name across the top of the paper—Willowdale Orphans Home, Bowling Green, Kentucky. Not Louisville, like she had always been told. And that was when she realized she could not trust her mother, she said—could not trust that anything they told her, or ever would tell her, was the truth about where she came from or who she was.

The corner of the paper hadn't been torn off the first time my mother found it, though she hadn't been able to read anything on it. The corner hadn't been torn off until the second time she snuck a peek.

The third time she went to look for the paper, she couldn't find it—her mother had hidden it somewhere else.

Elk Brand Mfg. Co.

My grandmother and my aunt work at the Elk Brand factory, where they make coats and overalls. My grandmother sews on pockets. My aunt runs a button-holer. Some of the overalls are striped, like an engineer's cap, and some are blue, like the kind my father got a new pair of every year for Christmas when he was growing up.

Elk Brand is an old square brick building downtown. It has three floors, with a long row of blacked out windows down the side of the top floor that look out over the roofs of the other buildings back down the street. Above the big glass front doors is a sign—Elk Brand Mfg. Co.—with a picture of an elk's head, with big horns.

My grandmother and aunt get off work at four o'clock, and we go and pick them up. My mother takes my sister and me, but leaves my brother home in case my great-grandmother wakes up or needs something.

We park on the street, as close to the factory doors as we can, to wait for them. My mother plays with my sister in the front seat. I sit in back. Sometimes I can climb up front, but not to fiddle with the car buttons.

Across the street from Elk Brand is a big vacant lot. You can see the train depot and the tracks on the other side, a row of old warehouses running a couple of blocks down that street.

The Elk Brand street is a couple of blocks of old factory buildings, a few houses between, stretching back to the milling company elevators and the old wooden water tower by the tracks, where the streets turn to go out of town.

Elk Brand is almost the last old factory. The others down the street— Mogul Wagons, Tandy Ice, Devil's Grip Tire Patch—are warehouses now or garages or empty. One of the old snuff factories is still running. The faded sign painted on the side of the brick building shows a big red snorting bull saying—

Chew Bull of the Woods

Brand

Cut Plug or Chew.

It's the kind my grandfather chews.

Waiting in the car, we watch the trucks and men coming and going at the warehouses, watch to see if a train comes through, and whether it stops at the depot if it does.

Then, at four o'clock, the women start coming out, out the big glass doors and down the big stone front steps, the younger ones, just girls, rushing out first, running down, like they were trying hard to be first. They go off down the street to find their rides, or stand around by the low stone wall that runs along the sidewalk and smoke and talk and wait.

My aunt is one of the first ones out, first to get to the car, so she can play with the baby in the front seat. She is always laughing and joking around and telling some story about something somebody did.

My grandmother comes out toward the end, with the older, slower women. She holds the railing going down the steps, and with every one, you can see the tops of her rolled-down stockings peek out from under her dress hem.

My grandmother sits in back with me. Her skin is always round and shiny, like the biscuit dough after she kneads it. A few twisty strands of gray hair have sprung loose from her hairpins.

She doesn't talk as much as my aunt. She's wearing the glasses I never see her wearing at home. She doesn't look like my grandmother until she takes them off.

*   *   *

A circus came through once and set up in the vacant lot across from Elk Brand. It was Moritz Bros.—Fourpaugh United Attractions. We saw the posters around town—they showed a tiger jumping through a ring of fire and a woman standing on a horse. We told my father about it, but he said we couldn't go—a show like that attracts too much riffraff, he said.

It took two days to set the circus up. We watched them those afternoons, waiting at Elk Brand. The first day, they unloaded the train cars that had pulled up on a side track, but we didn't see any animals. Then the second day, they were starting to put up the big striped tent, but we had to leave before they finished.

The next couple of nights, I could lie in bed and look out the window and see the big spotlight sweep around across the night sky, across the clouds and the darkness—my father told me the spotlight was at the circus, and that was how they advertised.

I watched it, the big tower of light, sweeping around the sky and wondered what it would be like, to be one of the circus men—pulling the big tent up, lifting it up in the air, see it rising in the sky. What it would be like to be old enough to be let to do that—some of the circus men looked like just boys—what it would be like—put up the big tent, take it down, then ride the train to the next stop. The things you could see.

"Think"—I told my mother that second afternoon, watching them work the tent up—"here we sit at Elk Brand every day and only see one circus, ever. But circus men ride the train and see a different Elk Brand everywhere they go."

West Side

The first house we lived in was at the top of McPherson Avenue hill, a block from where the street dead-ended, like all the streets on West Side did in that direction, at Todd's field, a cow pasture stretching on out of town, with an old brickworks on a back lot, down by the river.

I don't remember the house, but I have a photograph of my father sitting on the wood-plank back steps, screen door closed behind him. He's in a white undershirt, a cigarette in one hand, his other reaching to pet his two beagle hounds, clambering at his feet.

The second house we lived in was a block over, at the top of the street my grandmother and grandfather lived on. An alley ran behind it, with a crab apple tree at the edge of the yard. All the blocks on West Side had alleys running behind the houses, where trucks could go to deliver coal or clean out the outhouses, when there used to be outhouses.

Somebody left an old rusty swing set in the backyard. There was only one seat to swing on, but the teeter-totter worked o.k.

We had a little bulldog named Missy, and she died. We got two big boxer dogs named Huck and Auggie, after Huckleberry Hound and Auggie Doggie, the cartoons. I got stuffed animals of them for Christmas. Also, I got a Cape Canaveral set—it had astronauts and rockets, a launching pad and a control booth with some science guys.

That's when my sister was born. My mother brought her home and let me look at her. That would be my sister's first house.

The third house for me was a block down from that, closer to my grandmother and grandfather's. It was the biggest house we lived in. It had a long front porch, with a swing. It had a long back porch too, but we didn't live there long enough to unpack the boxes piled up back there, so we never got to play on it.

Huck and Auggie ran around in the vacant lot next door.

The alley ran all the way from behind our house to my grandparents', but you had to go by the bad house on the corner to get there. It was broke down and dirty, with no grass in the yard, just junk and bare dirt and a bunch of kids and babies running around in dirty diapers, and sometimes if one of the big kids saw you, they would stop you and ask for money.

When you walked down the alley, you could see into their house through a hole in the back wall, where somebody got drunk one night and blasted a shotgun at some of the kids.

Next we moved in with my grandmother, three blocks away. We lived in two rooms on one side, my grandmother and aunt in the two rooms on the other side, and then the kitchen. My great-grandmother lived with them too, but she mostly just lay in bed, so I didn't see her much.

The bathroom was built onto the back porch. The pipes weren't hooked up, so there was a sink but no water and a crusty old bag of white lime behind the door that you were supposed to throw a scoop full of down the toilet after you used the bathroom, but I didn't like touching it because my grandmother told me if you play with it, it will burn your skin off.

People took baths in the kitchen, sitting or standing in the tin wash tub my grandmother kept out on the porch. If it was winter, you could set the wash tub next to the stove, and she would turn on the oven and open the door, so you wouldn't freeze.

The coal shed was behind the old garage that nobody used, with just some rusty machine parts in one of the corners, weeds growing up through the gravel. I was the one sent out to fill up the coal bucket. It was old gray tin too, stamped on the side with a symbol and a name you could barely read—Dix Co. Clean Washed Coal.

I didn't like going out there. The coal shed was dark and smelled like old dirt and spiders.

That's where we lived when I started school. There wasn't room for dogs, so my father said he took the boxers to live with some people he knew out in the country.

When my father got his job driving the mail truck, we moved to Second Street, back toward my grandmother and grandfather's, just a block from school. The house backed up to a big, open lot. On one side was a man who kept a couple of mules in an old shed with a pen, and on the other was a man who kept a monkey in a chicken-wire cage he had built on the back of his garage, with a door for the monkey to go in and out.

We had seven cats there.

The last house we lived in was on Kentucky, down the street from Second Baptist Church. It was built like my grandmother's house, except we lived in all the rooms now. There was a pear tree in the back yard, with enough space for my father to grow a garden every year and for their two rat terrier dogs.

That was the house we lived in longest, six years. I graduated high school there. The summer after my first year away, I helped my mother and father move into the only house they would own, in one of the older subdivisions on the south side of town.

Their new street had been an old peach orchard—they had several trees in their back yard, others scattered across neighboring yards. They didn't clear a garden, but kept plants and flowers around the back porch. My mother planted wisteria to grow along the fence beside the house. For a while, my father grew a patch of roses, but burnt them all out at the roots one year when he thought he would use tobacco starter to fertilize them.

Shortly after they moved there, our old cat, Midnight, died—he had been with us since Second Street—and they buried him under one of the peach trees by the back fence.

A couple years later, I buried my parents' last little dog next to him, the last of their several fox terriers. I happened to be visiting the weekend she died, so I buried her for them that Sunday morning before I left.

World Book Encyclopedia

We had a set of World Book Encyclopedias, all black and white covers lined up in a row, with the alphabet.

A lady came to our house selling them. My mother and father knew her. She was an old school teacher. She came a couple of times, then my mother and father finally bought a set.

I liked the clear pages, where you could see all through the human body, and also the body of a frog. I liked the pages of Flags of the World and U.S. Presidents.

I looked up Kentucky, in J-K, and saw where we lived, with pictures of tobacco and horses and coal miners. Also, a picture of the world's largest steam shovel. We drove up to Muhlenberg County for a Sunday outing one time to see it, and I picked up a piece of coal for a souvenir, and there it was, a picture of it in World Book Encyclopedia.

The other books we had were a dozen hardbacks my mother always found a place to put out, whatever house we lived in. They were *The Silver Chalice*, *The Robe*, *PT-109*, like that. I think she belonged to Book-of-the-Month Club once, maybe a year. You see ads in the Sunday paper.

Also, the big family Bible that was always out on an end table or on top of the t.v. You could hardly pick it up, but there were a lot of pictures you could look at. The pages were all gold around the edges, and it had a white leather cover, with Jesus on the front.

Inside, the pictures were on the extra thick pages, printed in color on both sides. Sometimes, you knew the story of the picture, like Daniel in the Lion's Den or Moses Parts the Waters, but sometimes you didn't, so then you got to make up the Bible story yourself.

Bethel Baptist Church

Bethel Baptist Church sits next to the Jefferson Davis State Park and Monument, in Fairview, Kentucky, a few miles east of Hopkinsville. The church stands on the homesite of the house Davis was born in, which is why the monument is there.

Bethel Baptist was the first church my grandfather pastored full time.

When the church was dedicated, in 1886, Davis came up from Mississippi to attend the ceremony, but arrived several hours late because rain had muddied the roads, slowing the carriages that were bringing him and some other dignitaries down from the train station in Bowling Green.

Davis gave a short speech—from the floor, respecting the pulpit—and presented the congregation with a silver communion service—platter and chalice, with bowl and cups, inscribed to commemorate the occasion.

It was the set my grandfather used to celebrate the Lord's Supper when he was pastor there.

By chance, the last time I saw my grandfather preach was also the only time I saw him preach at Bethel Baptist Church. Long retired, he had been called on to substitute for the regular pastor that Sunday, on a weekend I happened to be visiting.

My mother and father and sister and I went to see him. His sermon that morning was not practiced or pointed, more casual and familiar, burnished remarks on a favorite text, *John* 3:16. He was delighted, though, with the surprise of our walking in as he was leading the service.

I have remembered that Sunday often, of course, for many reasons. And never do so without regretting that I did not ask my grandfather that day to show me that silver communion service.

★   ★   ★

My grandfather had worked on the Monument a couple of years, after he came back to Todd County from working out west. He mostly carried hod or drove the water wagon, but it was steady work for a while.

That too was when he met my grandmother. Her father had a farm in Fairview, and held a lamplighting at his house for some of the work crew one Saturday night. There was a fiddle player, and they drank early cider.

My grandfather would never have said so, but my grandmother told me there was also dancing.

*   *   *

Every year, on Confederate Memorial Day, there is a historical pageant at Jefferson Davis Park. Women wear hoop skirts, and men wear Confederate army uniforms. There are speeches and band music.

The Park picnic grounds are broad and shady. Church and scout groups go there, schools go for field trips.

Our family had what turned out to be our last two reunions there, the two years after my grandmother's last brother passed away and his old farmhouse sold, where we'd always had them before.

Then, with my grandmother passing two years after that, our last reunion at the Monument was the last time all the family was able to get together.

*   *   *

When he came back from the Army in 1926, my grandfather went to work in one of the woolen mills that was running at the time in Springfield, a few miles down the road, across the Tennessee line—where he was working when he got the call to preach.

The first few years, he served as a lay preacher, mostly substituting or leading revivals at different churches around the area, before being invited to pastor Bethel Baptist full time.

He couldn't be ordained, though, until he completed a year of Bible college. He was twenty-six years old, but had only finished three grades of school and couldn't read or write well enough to go.

So he started back at the fourth grade in Fairview's one-room schoolhouse, and went through sixth grade in one year, graduating Grammar School at age twenty-seven. He often told how cramped up he had gotten, trying to sit in the child-size school desks, and told how the children helped him with his lessons.

After Grammar School, the Bethel congregation raised a collection to send him to Chilhowee Bible Institute, in Chilhowee, Virginia, and he was ordained when he returned a year later.

At Bethel Baptist, my grandfather led a Christian Harmony singing school every summer, after taking the training for it in Bowling Green. One of the few photographs I have of him was taken at the side of Bethel Baptist Church, standing in front of one summer's solemn class, a few grave adults among the children, all clutching copies of the Stamps-Baxter Christian Harmony Singing School First Lesson Book, a copy of which I have managed to save.

*   *   *

After Bethel, my grandfather pastored several other churches briefly, before taking Bainbridge Grove Missionary Baptist, some fifteen miles west of Hopkinsville, where he served some thirty years before retiring.

For a while, he had a church in Central City, and on Saturdays he would drive up to some of the coal camps in Muhlenberg and hold Saturday services for the miners who worked Sundays.

My mother said she liked it when he let her and her mother go with him—she liked petting the blind mules that had been put to pasture, blind from working a lifetime in the underground darkness.

My mother said that many times my grandfather was paid with something other than money—food or garden vegetables or gas for his car. She rode home from church one night sharing the back seat with two live chickens in a pasteboard box—my grandfather's pay for conducting a week-long revival meeting.

My mother said she always looked forward to Sunday dinners after church, when they went to other peoples' houses to eat. Different people took the preacher's family home with them for dinner, and it was the only time during the week my mother knew she would get as much to eat as she wanted.

For many years, my mother's allowance was whatever pennies showed up in the collection plate on Sunday mornings. She knew that some Sundays, my grandfather would put a penny in himself.

But when they were at Salt Lick Church, in Logan County, old Miss Tandy learned about the arrangement, and afterwards my mother found pennies in the collection plate every Sunday, and sometimes a good many—enough, my mother said, to keep her in licorice and penny candy, even during war rations.

Later, she started saving her pennies, changing them into dimes and quarters, saving part of whatever other allowance she was given. Some of her coins she kept in a Smith Brothers Cough Medicine bottle under her bed. Her mother knew about that one, but she didn't know about the Waterman's Ink bottle with most of her money in it, tucked in a corner of her closet.

She was saving that in case her mother and father decided they wanted to take her back to the orphanage—she would have enough saved, she hoped, for a bus ticket to Hopkinsville, where she could go live with her Aunt Kitten and Uncle Terry.

*　　*　　*

The last time my mother saw her father, he didn't see her when she came into his room. He was in bed but awake, lying on his back.

Coming in, my mother paused in the doorway, watched him as he repeated the same slow gesture several times over—touching the fingertips of one hand to his chest, then lifting, turning his hand, opening his fingers out, as if releasing something into the air.

After watching him repeat the gesture several times—"Daddy," my mother said, "what are you doing?"

His hand continuing slowly to touch, lift, turn—"Putting the stars back in the heavens," he said.

Dry Branch

West Side ended, to the west, at Dry Branch, a muddy swamp that stretched out past the edge of town to a far patch of woods that backed up against the old drive-in movie theatre. A two-lane road skirted the edge of it, connecting the main road into town with another two-lane country road a couple miles north.

At the intersection, there was a big sinkhole that people used as a dump. In a heavy rain, the sinkhole flooded sometimes and washed trash up over the two-lane.

There was no road or path through Dry Branch—you either had to go around it or wade through it. People did now and then, mostly to go frog-gigging or to shoot turtles, but there were otherwise too many snakes and who knew what else—you'd hear rustling and snorting out in the cat-tails and weeds, or off in the trees, especially at night. You might hear a fox or a lost hound baying out somewhere on the far side of the woods.

A couple of the older kids said they found a path through Dry Branch once, that they rode their bikes down it and came to an old barn. There was nothing in it, they said, but there was an old well house too, and when they broke in the door and looked down in the well, it was just a dry pit, but there was a pile of bones at the bottom. They said they couldn't tell if the bones were human or not, but they probably were.

But then they wouldn't tell where to find the path, so most people didn't believe them. I think it could've been true, though.

*   *   *

The last house of West Side, before it ended, was the Clarks'. A long gravel drive led down a long, low hill to it, the drive sinking down below the back yards of the houses on the last paved street, down the hill and through some trees, the gravel part ending at their house. You could tell it had been an old farmhouse, from back when West Side was farmland. It was rundown and shabby, paint peeling off everywhere, showing a lot of gray boards underneath.

The house had a steep, rickety staircase leading down from the back porch to the long back yard that stretched down to the two-lane and Dry Branch on the other side. The side yard ended at a cornfield, which also ran all the way down to the two-lane.

The Clarks had the only yard closer than the park or the school that was big enough for baseball, so sometimes we played there. If we played in the evening, after supper, the air in the low bottom under the hill was cool and damp in the warm summer dusk, forming into low fog over Dry Branch, spreading, rising with the drone of the mudfrogs and katydids and nightjars.

When the big kids played, they always put me in the outfield—I couldn't catch well enough for infield, so they put me out next to the two-lane. Home plate was up at the back steps of the house. I always worried somebody would hit the ball across the road into Dry Branch, or even just into the cornfield, because I would be the one they sent in to get it, and you could never find it in either place, and also snakes—again, in both places.

You also had to hope nobody hit it off to the other side of the yard, where it would roll down the dirt part of the lane to the old run-down barn. There was nothing in it, but once in a while we'd see a tractor parked inside. Nobody knew who the barn or the tractor belonged to.

But everybody seemed to know that something bad happened in that barn. All the older kids seemed to know about it, and you'd hear them whispering.

But whatever it was, I could tell it was so bad that I never even wanted to ask my brother about it—I think because I didn't want to know what he would have told me, but also I didn't want to have to wonder forever whether it was true.

⋆   ⋆   ⋆

We were playing baseball there one afternoon when Mr. Clark came walking down the ditch by the two-lane in hip waders, rifle crooked in his arm, three squirrels dangling by their tails from his free hand. He'd been hunting in Dry Branch.

We stopped the game to watch him when he took the squirrels over to the side of the coal shed to dress them out. We all crowded up, watched him pin the back legs of one of them under his boots, cut a rim around the back side with his hunting knife, then pull the skin up, peeling, tearing it up over the neck and outstretched stumps of front legs, the liquid tearing of it, up over the bloody, naked gray meat underneath.

I only watched him do the first one, then waited by the side of the house until he finished, but everybody else watched him do all three, then walk over to the edge of the yard to throw the pan full of heads and guts off into the cornfield, then nail the skins up on the back wall of the shed, back where they used to keep chickens until the foxes kept getting them after their dog died.

Fire

One night after supper, we heard sirens down by Seventh Street, the main road into town through West Side. My father stepped out on the front porch to look, then out onto the sidewalk.

"One of the loose floors," he said, when he came back in.

We all went out on the sidewalk then, other people coming out too, some in pajamas already, all looking down the street at the huge yellow blaze lighting the sky in the direction of the river, four blocks away—a row of three or four tobacco warehouses on the other side of the river, down from the lumberyard—one of them on fire, maybe more.

It was October. The warehouses were full, most of them downtown, along the main train tracks, but others with spur tracks to them around different places too. You could smell the raw, acrid tobacco all over town that time of year. On Seventh Street, you'd see farmers bringing flat wagonloads of it in, piled in stacks of baskets, usually pulled by a truck or tractor, but once in a while by a team of old mules.

People started walking down the street toward the fire. There were more sirens, and now you could see some of the lights flashing red up against the sky.

Some people were clumped up in little groups at Second Street, but we followed a couple of others who kept on going, and then we were at Seventh Street, standing next to the church, and I was never allowed to go that close to the main road, not even with my brother.

The cars usually went pretty fast down there, but they were slowing down now so people driving by could look too, and now you have to bend your neck back to see the top of the blaze.

Then a couple of people go ahead and cross over between the slow cars, and we go with them, and I have never been on the other side of the big road before, and the sidewalk keeps going, and now we are walking down a street I didn't even know was here, and I am seeing houses I have never seen before and did not know were here, and cars and yards and things on people's porches, and dogs are barking somewhere, and the sirens all blaring back and forth are louder and louder, and now you can hear the fire too, and it's like a wind roaring and cracking, and the yellow light, lashing and flickering, is making shadows out of everything.

And then the sidewalk ends and then a patch of gravel, then grass, then people are crowded up, and you can even feel it now, hot crackling wind swirling up and over everything, and you can see more fire than sky now above us all.

And now my father is guiding me forward, behind me, hands on my shoulders, picking us a way through the clump of people, then I'm standing finally at the front, and it's only me out there, a little patch of grass, but right under me—

—the river, the river right under me, the grass dropping off two steps away down the bank to the dark water rippling by down there below. I have never been that close to the river before, either. My father's hands tighten on my shoulders.

And so I have emerged from the lashing shadows to stand alone at the river, nothing before me, to stand in the full light of the great blaze now, the heat of it washing over, have stepped for the first time beyond the edge of my world, have crossed over and seen the world beyond my world.

And it is burning.

Night Light

When you go downtown at night, you see a man made of lightning walking across the tops of the buildings, over top of all the roofs—even blocks away you can see him, white gloves on the ends of his lightning arms, his head a smiling face on a lit-up light bulb, a man made of lightning walking across the sky—then look, you see it's really Reddy Kilowatt, walking across a big billboard, saying out, in blinking lights—

. . . R—E—D—D—Y KILOWATT ! ! ! . . .

. . . AT YOUR SERVICE ! ! ! . . .

—except the exclamation points are lightning bolts.

Downtown

Going downtown, first is the Alhambra Theatre and the Sheriff's Office and the old Courthouse, past the little alley street with Inez's Beauty Shop, where sometimes my grandmother goes but sometimes not, then on down Main Street past some buildings we never go in, then it's the Hat & Dress Shop, then J.C. Penney's, which is two floors, and you can go up and down the big wide steps, or you can stand in the three-way mirror in the clothes aisle and look at a thousand of yourself.

Then comes the furniture store and then Woolworth's, with a popcorn machine near the checkout counter at the front, and in summer they open the double doors, and you can smell popcorn out on the sidewalk, and then there's the candy counter where you can buy bags of all different kinds, and then the 79-cent toy aisle and the aisle with the little ceramic bird statues my grandmother likes, and then some bigger toys, and over some of the aisles the big gray ceiling fans circle around slowly overhead, then in the back, getting closer you hear them, the parakeets and canaries chirping in their cages and the fountains of the fish tanks bubbling cool water.

Most times we walk, but when my grandfather drives us, he parks in front of Woolworth's and buys a bag of popcorn or candy and sits and eats it and watches people while he's waiting for us. Sometimes at church on Sunday morning, he tells about something he saw or saw somebody do.

Then on down there's Kress's, like Woolworth's except not as good, they have o.k. toys, but it's mostly clothes. Then the bank at the big intersection and on up the street is Ferrell's hamburgers, which is just a little room with a counter and a few stools and a room in the back off the alley where black people can eat.

Then across the street is the big hardware store with the toy section on the second floor and the only elevator in town you can ride. There's a mechanical pony up there too, you can ride for a quarter. In back, downstairs, is the big scale where they weigh bags of seeds or nails and you can stand on it and weigh yourself too, but they don't like you to do it, so you wait until nobody's back there.

Then back down Main Street there's Montgomery Ward that my father always calls Monkey Ward's and smells like rubber tires when you go in. They don't have many toys, but upstairs are the bicycles, where my father brought me and my brother to buy new ones after we moved out of my grandmother's, and where my grandfather bought new ones for us after those got stolen.

Then there's the little jewelry store with moving displays in the window. At Christmas, it's Santa and the elves and the Christmas train, going around. At Easter, it's bunnies and chicks popping out of Easter eggs.

Then, at the big intersection again is the shoe store we go to for school shoes, and they give you a balloon to take home, and across the street is Men & Boys Store we go to for new school clothes, which I hate because the guy is always poking at you with his tape measure and jerking your waist around and looking at you.

Then there's the other hamburger place, but my grandmother doesn't like to go there because they have a pool room in back, and she doesn't like the looks of the people that go in and out back there.

Then Rexall Drugs where my grandmother stops almost every time, then back up the hill past the other bank and the office supply store you go to every year with your list for school, but they don't like seeing you in there if you go in without your mother.

Then the other hardware store, but they don't have anything for kids so nobody goes there. It's the store my father's father worked at, after they moved to town, before he died.

Then back to the Courthouse again. Across from it is a little brick building painted blue, backing up to the used car lot around the corner. Painted on the window is a picture of a man's scary face looking out behind prison bars.

The neon sign above the door says—
CARR'S BAIL BONDS
Licensed
24 H URS
TUxedo 6-5893.
If you're wondering what a HUR is, it really says 24 HOURS, but the O is always burned out.

Illinois Central Freight Depot

Little River skirts along the west side of town. The Illinois Central freight depot was an old wood-frame warehouse that stretched some two city blocks along the town side of the river. On the other side, across from the depot, was West Side Park.

We never lived more than five blocks from there. I would lie awake at night and listen to the trains coming and going at the depot—the boxcars coupling and uncoupling, the screech and squall of the wheels and the brakes.

When I was older, freight trains weren't stopping there anymore. They passed on through to Nashville, so the depot wasn't being used anymore, either. And it had become a bad place.

Winos and old bums hung around there. The ground was scattered with trash and whiskey bottles and dirty newspapers. We were told to always cross to the other side of the street if we walked by.

You could see inside, through a couple of big, open doorways, but it was dark and shadowy in there. You could make out piles of stuff in the corners, blankets or old clothes, and sometimes, somebody moving around.

Pigeons flew in and out.

Once, when we were walking into town with my grandmother, we came across two men fighting there, on the river bank behind the depot. My grandmother chased one of the men off, but the other one sat on the ground with blood and dirt on his face and on his ripped shirt. My grandmother asked him if he needed help. He just looked at her and cussed her and told her we didn't need to know his business.

West Side was an old park, and the only one on that side of town. To go in, you walked under a gray stone arch with the name carved on it. You came to a big round pit, surrounded by a low stone wall, that used to be a fish pond. From there, stone paths led off in different directions, to a picnic ground with shade trees and tables, to a playground with shuffleboard and horseshoes.

The baseball field was down by the river.

This is where we played Park League games. We were the West Side Rockets. We had yellow caps and blue t-shirts, with a rocket ship on the front. Some of the other teams were the Indian Hills Chiefs, the Millbrook Bulldogs, and the Crispus Attucks Hawks.

Hopkinsville once had a professional baseball team, in a league—the Hoptown Hoppers. Bill Monroe brought his tent show to town once and set it up in West Side Park. On the afternoon before the show, the Bluegrass Boys played a game of baseball against the Hoptown Hoppers on the West Side field. It was in the newspapers.

The freight depot was across the river from left field. A couple of old boxcars still sat on the tracks there. Sometimes, when we played our games, one or two old guys from the freight depot would come down to watch us. Sometimes they would climb on top of the boxcars, where they could get a good view. Once in a while, one of them would yell something at us, but mostly they just watched, and maybe passed a paper bag with a bottle back and forth.

One night there was a fire at the freight depot. You could see the flames from all over West Side. The fire was only in one end of the building, and they were able to put it out before it spread, but we found out the next day that an old man sleeping inside got burned up.

Not long after that, bulldozers came in and tore the whole depot down. For two blocks, it was a giant pile of timber and bricks and trash. It was like that for nearly a year, before they finally hauled it all off.

I wrote one of the first poems I can remember about it. I was thirteen:

Illinois Central Freight Depot

They're tearing down the refuge
For the old
Drunkmen,

And Lord
It never even
Got a fair trial.

["Drunkmen," *sic*]

The Kentucky Club

My mother was in high school when they moved to Hopkinsville. It was the biggest town any of them had lived in.

My grandmother's sister had moved there before the war, when her husband bought the tavern on First Street that he ran the rest of his life, The Kentucky Club. A neon sign over the door showed a playing card, an ace, with the words—

Kentucky Club
The Ace of Clubs.

It was on a two-block-long stretch of bars people called Skid Row. There was also a pawn shop, and a shoe-shine stand outside a run-down barber shop, and a used furniture store. The windows of all the bars were all blacked out so you couldn't see in.

When you drove through, you always saw a couple of ragged looking old men sitting out on the sidewalk or sleeping in a doorway.

Around one corner was the Jewish department store that, for a long time, was the only department store in town where black people could shop. Around another corner was a drugstore with a pool hall in the basement, where my father learned to shoot pool after they moved to town.

I tried to picture him as one of the tough-looking guys with tattoos, smoking cigarettes, that you always saw hanging around the drugstore corner by the basement stairs.

*   *   *

My mother's cousin was the same age, so they finished high school together. She was the closest my mother had to a sister. She had moved away before I was born, but I knew Uncle Terry and Aunt Kitten, short for Kathleen. Uncle Terry always wore a suit and tie. Aunt Kitten always wore make-up and big jewelry and smelled like perfume.

They lived in a nice house in an old part of town. I was always afraid to touch things when we went there. A black woman named Ella came to clean their house for them. Ella only had one eye, and she was really nice, and sometimes she would come and help at my grandmother's house when my grandmother was sick.

Aunt Kitten worked for a while at a store downtown called The Hat & Dress Shop. When my grandmother took me with her to Inez's Beauty Shop, we would sometimes stop in and see her.

Inez's Beauty Shop had a sign on the door that said—
U—R Welcome!
Walk In!
At Inez's, I sat and watched my grandmother talk to the other women and get her hair washed. It was always noisy, with the big helmet dryers running, and it smelled bad, but kind of sweet too, but there were magazines to look at, and sometimes my grandmother would let me get a Dr. Pepper out of the machine.

At the Hat & Dress Shop, while my grandmother and Aunt Kitten talked, I mostly looked at hats.

*   *   *

My grandfather and Uncle Terry were best of friends. Every summer, for many years, they drove to Florida together for a vacation, sometimes taking their families, sometimes not. I have a photograph of them fishing together off a pier at Daytona Beach.

What differences they may have had, preacher and tavern owner, seem not to have been of matter. Terry never drank around my grandfather, of course, and I only heard my grandfather say once of Uncle Terry's business that he "earned an honest living" at what he did.

But my mother once overheard a conversation between them, my grandfather saying, "Terry, you know where you're going to end up if you don't stop that drinking," Terry answering, "Well Preacher, I'd rather end up there than to spend all eternity listening to a bunch of old women complain about their ailments."

*   *   *

My mother said Uncle Terry always treated her as much like his own daughter as he did her cousin.

She said he was known to have a temper, though she rarely saw it, and he always carried a pistol, but she'd never heard of him using it. She said he especially "hated meanness," and said she had heard stories that he once beat a man in the alley behind his tavern after he saw the man kick a dog.

My mother said he was always generous, more so when he'd been drinking. One night she was sleeping over at their house, and Uncle Terry came home late, woke her and her cousin up to hand my mother a Kentucky Club envelope with five one-hundred-dollar bills in it, instructing her to "tell that skinflint Baptist daddy of yours he doesn't know what a good daughter he's got."

Her cousin slipped the money back in his wallet before he woke up the next morning.

Another time, Uncle Terry had given my mother ten dollars, and when her mother found out about it, made her go and give the money back to him.

When she did, Uncle Terry took it and said, "So your mother doesn't think I should have given you ten dollars?"—put the ten in his wallet, took out a hundred-dollar bill, gave it to her, and said, "You tell your mother you gave me back that ten dollars, and I sure appreciate it."

My mother said this time she kept the money.

Wreck of the Titanic

My grandmother had an old phonograph, the kind with a crank you turn. It was a big cabinet that stood in the corner of the living room next to the coal grate. The bottom of the cabinet was a big drawer that pulled out with all the old thick, black records inside.

They bought the phonograph when they were still on the farm, from a man who was going around the county selling them off the back of a wagon. The records in the drawer came with it.

We children were not let to play with the phonograph, or even touch the crank, only my grandmother. And she only played it once in a while, on Sunday afternoons after Sunday dinner, if we asked her enough times.

She kept a lace doily and a little blue glass bowl on top of it, to keep us from opening the lid. The bowl she got from a box of Crystal Wedding Oats.

First, my grandmother set those off on the mantle, then carefully lifted the lid, propped it open, then sat in the caned chair next to it to work the machinery.

Sometimes she let one of us give the crank a turn or two, but mostly it was her, and when she cranked it up enough, she set the needle down on the spinning black plate, and the old-timey music came scratching out of the speaker hidden behind the fancy carved front of the cabinet.

She only played two records, the first two in the big drawer, which she had to have one of us children pull out because it was too heavy for her.

The first record she put on was the funny one—she let us dance around and joke and sing along to it. It was called "Don't Bring Lulu." It told about somebody going to a party, about who they could bring with them and who they couldn't—

> You can bring Rose
> With the rubber nose,
> But don't bring Lulu.

> You can bring Peg
> With the wooden leg,
> But don't bring Lulu.

No don't bring Lulu.
She's wild as a Zulu.
Don't bring
Don't bring Lulu.

My grandmother laughed along with that one too, watching us dance around, patting her twisted fingers on her knees in time with the music. But then for the second record we had to stop dancing around and had to sit quiet and listen, like in church, like she did when she played it.

It was "Wreck of the Titanic." The label showed two angels in white robes and white wings, blowing long trumpets into the air over the words. The other side of the record showed the same two angels blowing their trumpets over "What Mother's Child Lay Sleeping Here?"

When my grandmother put the second record on and started turning the crank again, we knew it was time for us children to sit down and get quiet—she wouldn't set the needle down until we did—

It was sad when that great ship went down,
Sad when that great ship went down.

Husbands and their wives,
Little children lost their lives.
It was sad when that great ship went down.

Also on the mantle, a little wooden house painted pink and blue with two doors—if it's going to rain, the little boy with the pointed hat and green suspenders comes out the blue door, and if it's going to be sunny, the little girl in the blue dress and a flower in her hair comes out the pink one.

I don't know where my grandmother got the little wooden house.

Bristol

Four years my father spent in the Navy. Much of it on tour in the Mediterranean—Athens, Rome, Gibraltar—and he talks more about his train trips to Norfolk, Virginia, where he was based, than about the whole rest of the time he spent on the other side of the world.

Uncle CC always drove him to the station, in time for them to stop at the liquor store across the tracks for a pint of Four Roses for my father to slip in his pocket for the trip.

The first time my father left to go overseas, Uncle CC told him to be careful, that there were probably a lot of places out in an ocean where a fellow could drown. My father told him, "Goddamnit, CC, you sound like Mama. It ought not be any easier to drown in an ocean than it would be anyplace else. All it takes is a lungful, no matter where you are."

The first time my father came home in his sailor's suit, Uncle CC made him stop at the photo booth in Higgins Drug Store and get his picture taken. It's one of the few photographs I have of him in uniform.

On the train out of Nashville, my father would meet other boys on their way to Norfolk. They'd be from all over—Kansas, Mississippi, Oklahoma. After he'd been in for a while, he'd pick out the new recruits to talk to, make up things to tell them about the Navy that would scare them even more than they already were.

On one trip, he played blackjack in the club car with a one-armed man. The man could shuffle and deal, all with his one hand. On another trip, there was an old woman smoking a long-stemmed pipe. They had to put her off in Knoxville for being drunk and disorderly.

On another, a black man tried to get on in Roanoke with a cardboard suitcase and a scythe. They wouldn't let him bring his scythe on with him, and he wouldn't let them put it in the baggage car, so he ended up not riding.

One of the places my father would change trains was Bristol, Tennessee— or Bristol, Virginia. The state line runs through the middle of town, half of it in one state, half in the other.

My father would go and eat supper in a cafe at the end of the main street. The cafe was split down the middle too, with a white line painted across the floor and up the walls—one side in Tennessee, the other in Virginia.

Once, when I was little, and he was telling this, I asked him which side he liked best.

"The Tennessee side," he said, after thinking a minute. "Tennessee sounds somewhat closer to home than Virginia."

Twilight Speedway

Twilight Speedway was on a side of town we didn't go to much until my grandmother moved over there. It was a dirt racetrack with a dirt lane leading off the highway to it. A sign by the road showed a checkered flag and the race times. Sometimes they had demolition derbies.

We went to a race once, at night—a memory too early to be clear, but vivid still: the plank-and-cinderblock seats, the smell of burnt oil and car smoke, aftershave and beer and popcorn, the different-colored cars, painted with numbers and names I couldn't read, all dirt-caked and browned over, blatting around the curves, the red dust rising up from the blur and the noise, hazing the spotlights spaced around the track, eyes on poles, gazing their light down on the cars and the drivers going on and on and on, around and around below.

*   *   *

My mother told me once that, when he worked at the sheet metal shop, my father got paid on Saturday afternoon, and sometimes on his way home he would stop by the running craps game that met most Saturdays under the Twilight Speedway bleachers.

She said my father used to be a pretty good gambler, that several times when the police raided the game, he had already won enough to pay his fine and go ahead and get out of jail and not have to spend the night, like some of his friends. She said he still made it home before supper, even on those afternoons.

She told me once, too, that one of his first jobs was working with Uncle CC, driving used cars from some dealer in town to some place in Jackson, Tennessee. They would drive two cars down and bring one or two back, or sometimes take the bus back.

My mother said the talk around town had it that as many of that dealer's cars were stolen as were "used." She said she still wasn't sure if my father was old enough to have his driver's license at the time.

*   *   *

My father was building us a go-cart at his shop. He was making it out of scraps and pieces of metal and pipe, leftovers from different jobs, working on it when he wasn't busy or during his lunch. He took me and my brother there one Saturday afternoon to look at it, the only time I was in his shop.

He let us in through a side door. It smelled like old grease and metal, rust and grime and blacked over machines, oil cans and caked-up rags. The light switch clanked on loud when my father pushed it, and the big lights overhead popped when they came on.

Over in a corner of the shop was the go-cart. My father showed us how it was going to look, after he got all the pieces put together. You could see where the wheels would go, and the seat and the motor. You could see how the steering wheel would be connected. There was going to be a roll bar.

Not long after that, though, the shop closed, and we moved in with my grandmother, so my father didn't get to finish our go-cart.

*   *   *

We went to see Ace Denny's Auto Thrill Show at the Fairgrounds.

The drivers did stunts. They drove donut circles and figure eights in the dirt. They drove around the track on two side wheels, then raced each other going backward.

There was a clown on a motorcycle. And then another clown in a little truck.

Then Ace Denny stood on top of one of the cars in a crash helmet and the car came fast down the track and jumped up a ramp and up through a giant ring of fire and landed down on the other side and then the people ran out to see if Ace Denny was o.k. and he was o.k.

*   *   *

Sometimes on Sunday afternoon, we drive out to Tongate's Drive-In for ice cream cones. You sit in your car and they come out and ask for your order then bring your ice cream or your hot dogs out to you.

Sometimes on the way home, we go by the salvage yard to see if any new wrecked cars have been brought in over the weekend. The wrecks are left sitting in front of the gate, waiting to be towed in when the yard opens Monday morning.

Sometimes we pull in and look at one, if it's really bad, but usually we just slow down and look at them as we drive by and finish our ice cream on our way home.

*   *   *

My father bought my brother and me a big plastic model of a car engine to put together. When you finished it and hooked it up to a battery, it really worked. The outside was clear, so when you got it running you could see what made a car motor go.

It took us a long time to build. But my father helped some, and when we finished, he showed us what all the pieces were and how they work together, how the spark plugs explode the gas and drive the pistons, how the crankshaft pumps and turns, what the belts and flywheels do.

We lost track of the model engine in one of our moves, after we'd had it a couple years. Most of what I know about cars, though, I learned from it.

*   *   *

Memorial Day was one of the holidays my father didn't have to work, and it was also his birthday. And it was the day of the Indianapolis 500. Every year we listened to it.

In the days before the race, we read the paper to see who was in it that year. Some years I wrote a list of all the drivers, for us to use when the race came on.

Most years, we just listened to it on the radio in the kitchen. We sat around the table and got ready to hear them say, "Gentlemen, start your engines," and all listened a while for some of the early laps. Then we drifted in and out of the kitchen, different ones of us listening off and on, as the race went on.

Sometimes my father helped me keep up with my list—we marked who was winning and marked people off when they wrecked or broke down.

Some years, though, when the weather was nice, we went fishing on Memorial Day. We usually drove out to somebody's farm he knew, with a pond in a cow field or a tractor path down to a creek. My father would pull the car in through the weeds or trees or across a field, to get as close to the water as he could, so we could keep the radio on and the car windows down and listen to the race while we fished.

After he got us started, my father let my mother help me and my brother fish while he moved down the bank to fish more by himself.

He used the fishing rod that had belonged to his father. My father kept it in the trunk of the car, and sometimes when we were out somewhere and he saw a good spot and he had time, we would pull over and he would get it out and we'd fish with it a few minutes.

On Memorial Day, he took it and worked his way down the pond bank or creek bank a ways, far enough where he was just still able to hear the radio, so he could stand and cast and reel and listen to the race—the cars burring by, the announcers telling what happened, who crashed and who was in the lead, how many laps there are to go.

*　　*　　*

The only car my father bought new was a 1966 Pontiac GTO. It was red, with real wood on the dashboard and two front seats with a gear shift in the floor between them so nobody could sit in the middle. He bought it after he got a new mail route, one that kept him closer to home, and my mother went back to work.

That summer, before my sixth grade, we went on the one big vacation we took. We drove to Washington, D.C. and stayed in a hotel. It took a day and a half to get there. We got there at night, and drove by the Iwo Jima statue, with the soldiers raising the big flag, all lit up.

In Washington, we saw the Washington Monument and the Lincoln Memorial. We went in museums and saw the Declaration of Independence and Old Glory and the Spirit of St. Louis—one museum had actual rocket ships standing in the street beside it. We took tours of the Capitol and then the White House, where you couldn't touch anything, and you surely could not get off the strip of red carpet that ran through all the rooms.

Coming home, we spent the night in a hotel in the Smoky Mountains. The next day, before heading back, we took a ride on a genuine steam train. We had seen signs for it—

Travel Back in Time!

On Great Smoky Mtn. Railway!

—with a picture of the train.

There were signs for other places—Lost World, City of Wonder! and Underground Boat Rides in Crystal Caverns! and Chief Cherokee Trading Post!

—that sign showed teepees.

They all looked good, but we let my mother pick. And she picked Travel Back in Time! Great Smoky Mtn. Railway!

★   ★   ★

The GTO was the last car my father bought. He drove it until it was no longer drivable, and by then was driving his truck most of the time anyway.

He had kept the GTO up and running for a good while. My sister and I each drove it a couple of years, even, when we were between cars.

Finally, to get it out of the driveway, my father pulled it up beside the house, where, over the years, it went to ruin. I asked him many times to sell it to me, to let me fix it up, make it drivable again, but he never would.

My father lost his driver's license when he had his first seizure. About a year later, he sold the GTO to some guy he didn't know for salvage. The guy had been driving by and saw it sitting beside the house. He paid my father $200 for it, came back with a wrecker and towed it away.

★   ★   ★

Among the few things he left, I have not been able to find my father's fishing rod, the one that had belonged to his father, the grandfather I did not know.

I couldn't have missed it—there weren't that many things.

It was likely still in the trunk of the GTO, where he always kept it.

Brass Eagles

My mother showed me an old banjo that had been my father's. She kept it in a closet with his leather hunting coat and his things from the Navy. I had never seen it before.

The banjo's head was missing, and there were no strings—it was just the tarnished metal rim with a crude, hand-carved wooden neck.

Mounted around the rim, though, was a row of small brass eagles, wings unfurled, burnished dark gold. There would have been thirteen of them, but one had been knocked off.

When my father was a boy, his father had given him one of the piglets from a new litter to raise for his own and eventually sell to market and have the money to keep.

Instead, my father took his pig and traded it for the banjo. It belonged to an old man who lived down the road from them. My father would go down and listen to the old man play, and liked the banjo so much he finally talked the old man into trading for it.

My mother said my father never learned to play it himself, though.

The Blue Rose

Over his life, my grandfather did a lot of different things for money—he never made enough as a preacher until his last church finally grew big enough to pay him a steady enough salary.

When he was younger, he just worked at whatever job he could find. When he was still traveling, before he joined the Army, he even made things out of scrap wood—milking stools or birdhouses or shoe-shine boxes—and sold them on the street, or went door to door with them. He made one-string guitars, out of cigar boxes and sticks of wood—to play one, you lay it on your lap, pluck the string with a pick, and use an aspirin bottle for a slide. He sold those on the street too.

When my mother was growing up, he ran a used furniture store during the time they lived in Central City. Every few months, he would drive his truck to Chicago for a new load of furniture to bring back and sell. He tried to plan his trips so he could go to Sunday morning service at the Dwight Moody tabernacle, downtown in Chicago, a service he sometimes listened to on the radio at home.

When they first moved to Hopkinsville, my grandfather and grandmother ran a lunch counter downtown for a while, and later, when I was growing up, he ran a shoe repair shop.

The thing he did longest was to work on pianos, tuning and repairing and rebuilding them. He learned how from a man they shared a house with when they lived in Russellville. The man was blind and had learned piano work at a school for the blind. His son, who had driven his car for him and helped him in his business, had gone into the Army and was overseas fighting the war, so the man hired my grandfather to drive for him and ended up teaching him the trade.

After they'd been in Hopkinsville a few years, my grandfather opened a piano shop in a side street storefront downtown, where he repaired and sold used pianos. The store's front was a door and, next to it, a big display window, big enough for my grandfather to put a piano there for advertising. Some afternoons, or on Saturdays, my mother would go down to the store and play the piano in the window for a while, for more advertising.

That's where my father first saw her. He was just home from the Navy, downtown on a Saturday afternoon, walked by, heard the music and stopped to watch my mother in the window, playing piano.

He said he didn't know who she was, didn't know how he would ever meet her, but knew from that first time he saw her that he was going to marry her.

⋆   ⋆   ⋆

My father was nineteen when he joined the Navy, a few months after his father died.

They had moved to town when he was fourteen, when their tobacco barn burned down. They didn't have money to rebuild it and, without tobacco, couldn't live off what else they could grow on such a small farm, so had to sell out and move to town.

My grandmother went to work at Elk Brand, my grandfather at one of the hardware stores downtown, where he worked the five years before he died. When he worked there, the hardware store still sold coffins—it showed them in the newspaper ads.

My father tried school in town but didn't like it. He went mostly regularly when they lived in the country, but quit before Christmas that first year in town—his eighth grade—and didn't go back.

He picked up different jobs around town after that, delivering groceries or loading trucks or painting houses. For a while he bagged groceries at the Red Front Grocery, across from the railroad depot, where he made sandwiches and brought them over to sell to people on the trains that stopped.

His brother was older and helped him find work—CC got him a job cleaning out taxicabs, and they worked together for a while for a used car dealer in town. Some years later, CC was already driving a truck for the post office and helped my father get his first mail route, to Evansville, after the sheet metal shop closed. What time my father wasn't working, he spent hanging around the pool hall in the basement of Higgins Drug Store.

My father doesn't talk about those years, even less than about others. What I know of them, I know mostly from my mother. She also told me that the rumors around town were that a lot of the cars CC and my father handled for that dealer were stolen, and that the "Al" of Al's Radio Cabs was bootlegging whisky out of those taxis my father had been paid to "clean out."

My mother said she didn't know whether any of that was true, or whether my father was any part of any of it, but there may be reasons he doesn't have much to say about that time—a time that was hard enough as it was, with his father being sick during most of those years before he finally died.

She did say, though, that my father admitted to being in with the group of kids that burned down McKee's lumber yard south of town and never got caught—one of them had gotten hold of a stick of dynamite, and they took it out there to set it off, blew the back wall out of a drying shed, and ended up burning the whole lumberyard to the ground before they could get the fire put out. My mother said the police asked my father some questions, but none of them was ever arrested.

She told me that, and that he always did love gambling.

When he enlisted, my father was sent to Chicago, took the train to the Naval Station there for basic training. That was the farthest he'd ever been from home, and where he learned to swim. He went to Cook School and learned how to bake. Then he was stationed at Norfolk, with a supply ship that toured the Mediterranean a couple times while he was on it.

My father brought back a handful of postcards and coins from Greece and Italy, which he kept in a tin box in a dresser drawer, along with his Service papers and Navy Class Book, his feathered and ragged New Testament, and his rusted pistol with the bullets in a glass jar.

He had been home from the Navy less than a year when he was walking downtown one Saturday afternoon, cut through a side street on his way to the movie theatre, and passed by the storefront window where my mother was playing piano. They were married the year after.

★   ★   ★

After high school, my mother went to the Women's College in town for a semester—I remember her saying she enjoyed Home Ec and Glee Club—before she quit to marry a boy who lived down the street from them and had gone to high school with her. He was from a somewhat better-off family, and my grandparents liked him a lot.

He enlisted in the Army after my brother was born, a year after they were married. When he finished training and was stationed in Boston, my grandparents begged my mother to stay home with them and let them help her take care of the baby, but she wanted to go, so she did.

She said she never knew the boy drank until they moved to Boston, and it got worse the longer they stayed. They'd been there a year when he hit her the one time, she called my grandparents and told them she wanted to come home.

My grandfather told her to take the train to Washington, D.C.—as far as he would go to pick her up to bring her back.

My mother said she left my brother's father, and Boston, the week before Christmas, by calling a taxi from the phone in the boarding house hallway to take her and my brother to the train station.

She said she knew she had enough money for the train ticket, but knew she didn't have enough for cab fare all the way to the station. She figured she would go as far as she could pay to go, then just have to walk the rest of the way. She sat in the back seat, where she could watch the taxi meter click off the fare, and when it got close to how much she had, she told the driver to pull over, that was as far as she could pay to go.

The driver asked her if that was all the money she had, and when she told him all but train fare, he took her and my brother the rest of the way to the station, then wouldn't let her pay him.

It was a four-day trip, Boston to Washington, then the drive back to Hopkinsville. They got back home two days before Christmas.

My mother had only been back in Hopkinsville a few months, that Saturday afternoon she was playing piano in the storefront window, when my father cut through a side street on his way to a movie.

*   *   *

A little over a year after he was discharged from the Navy, my father was drafted into the Army. It wasn't supposed to happen, but it did, and they made my father stay in the Army for two years anyway.

They stationed him at Camp Breckinridge, Kentucky, some sixty miles away. He drove back and forth to Hopkinsville on weekends—once, as he told it, through rain with no windshield wipers and his head stuck out the window to see. In the Army, at Breckinridge, is where he learned sheet metal work.

The first place my father and mother and brother lived was an apartment over somebody's garage, down the street from my grandparents. Then they lived a few months in a house downtown, by the hospital, before moving back to West Side and the house at the top of McPherson hill, where they were living when I was born.

*　　*　　*

I was in high school when I found out my brother had a different father, and I found out the same time he did.

My brother had already married and moved out. His father was living in Indiana, had gotten in touch with my grandparents and told them he wanted to see his son. They told my mother, let her be the one to tell my brother, tell him the whole story of it—let her be the one to give him the choice of meeting his father or not. She did, and he decided that he did, very much, want to meet.

His father came down to Hopkinsville then, spent several days with my brother and his wife. They got on well and, after that first meeting, he and my brother visited each other a number of times over the next several years, before he passed away.

He had stayed in the Army, been stationed around the world—England, Germany, the Philippines—retired from the service to Indiana, gone into business, then retired from that. He had remarried, but his second wife had passed away, and they'd had no children.

Some time later, my mother told me that, several times over the years, he had gotten in touch with her, or tried to, with letters or phone calls, always through my grandparents—asking her to come back to him, to take my brother and leave my father and come be with him, wherever he was at the time.

She didn't tell anything else that passed between them, only that she finally wrote him one letter in response, and that she hadn't heard from him since—and that had been some years before—until he had called, wanting to see my brother.

She knew she couldn't stand in the way of that. She went to my brother's house that same afternoon to tell him, then told my sister and me the next morning.

*   *   *

I was five, maybe four, when I found the toy car at my grandparents' house. It was still in its box, stuffed in the back of a kitchen drawer full of old towels my grandmother never used. The box showed a picture of the car, with writing in a language I couldn't read, but knew was not English.

The car was red, shiny metal, heavy and big as my two hands when I pulled it out, with a little man in a hat driving it, and a key sticking out the back you could wind it up with.

There were no toys at my grandparents' house, except the ones we might bring then take back home with us when we left. And this was the nicest toy I had ever seen, nicer than anything you'd ever see in a store, or even in a catalog.

I could not imagine where such a toy car could have come from.

When my grandmother came in and saw I had found it, she told me to be careful, but let me set it down on the floor and wind it up. You could move the steering wheel to make the car go any direction you wanted, even around in big circles, and the little man looked like he was driving it.

I wound it up and made him drive around the kitchen floor, across and around the the shiny, cool linoleum, the pink and black checkerboard, under the table and around the legs and around and around through the chair legs.

After letting it run down that once, my grandmother picked the toy car up, put it back in its box, put the box back in the drawer, stuffed the old towels back in front, and told me I was never to touch it again. So, of course, I never asked about the toy car again, either.

Over the years, I did, though, sneak another peek or two at the box, once even opening it enough to pull the car out as far as its front wheels, then quickly shutting the box and drawer before I got caught. Those were the only two times I ever saw the car itself.

I hadn't thought of the toy car for many years, until long after my mother had told me the story of her first marriage, when it occurred to me that the language on the box was German, that the car was likely something my brother's father had sent to him from overseas. I could understand, then, why it was kept at my grandparents' house instead of ours.

But I did wonder how it had come to be there—whether my brother's father had sent it first to my grandparents, or to my mother, whether my brother had even seen it. Or whether, even, as was certainly possible, he had been allowed to play with it at my grandparents' house when I wasn't there—something he never mentioned, but wouldn't have.

*   *   *

On the inside of my father's left calf was a tattoo of a woman in a bathing suit, arms over her head, as if dancing, a rose gripped in her teeth, all in blue ink, the name—Lila—lettered out underneath her, also in blue.

Lila was the girlfriend my father had before he went into the Navy. He never mentioned her, of course, and I never learned where he got the tattoo. My mother told the story that Lila was originally naked, but after they got married, she made my father go back down to the tattoo parlor to have some clothes put on her, a story my father never confirmed but would not deny.

If my father sat with his legs crossed, and his pants cuff rode up above the top of his sock, Lila would sometimes show a bit, more or less of her head and arms and body. Whenever my mother would see it, she would tell him he needed to cover Lila up, and make him pull his pants leg down. In church, especially, she would make one of us children nudge him and tell him.

We heard her say to him once that everybody in that church knew about him and Lila, there was no need for him to advertise it.

Over time, the ink faded, and my father's leg drew smaller, but Lila remained, and distinctly so—frequently, the only thing emerging, visible between my father's cuff and sock, being the blue rose, blooming in Lila's teeth.

And I came, over time, in later years, to stop telling him, stop nudging him to pull his pants leg down, to cover Lila up. I had been neglecting to do this for some time, and purposely so, before I thought to question why, then came to understand—I had come to do this not to embarrass or shame him, but in fact, the opposite: I had taken to leaving Lila, her blue rose, uncovered and dancing, from gratitude and respect for the few stories of my father's life that have been revealed to me, but, more, to honor all those that have not.

Christmas, Bainbridge Grove
Missionary Baptist Church

We only go to church at night two times a year, for Christmas in winter and Vacation Bible School graduation in summer.

At Bible School graduation, the kids wait outside until we're told to line up and march in. It's just getting dark by then, and you can hear the creek running behind the church, and all across the field and pastures around the church house you can hear the mudfrogs and katydids and nightjars starting up for the night.

When you get inside even, you can still hear them through the open windows, can hear the moths scritching at the screens, if you sit at the end of a pew.

At Christmas, it's always cold inside the church, and a lot of people keep their coats on. And it always seems dark, darker than in summer, even though all the same lights are on, and there's even a lit-up Christmas tree in the corner.

Christmas service is the same every year. There's special singing first. The old song leader, Mr. Overby, leads us all in some Christmas carols. Mr. Overby is in his nineties and still farms a patch of tobacco and walks the mile and a half from his house to church every Sunday morning, but lets people drive him on Sunday nights.

Then the Hale sisters sing Beautiful Star of Bethlehem—the only time I ever hear that song. Only two of the sisters go to our church. The other two are Methodists and go to church on the other side of the hill from our church, so Christmas is the only time we see them.

One of the Methodist sisters is round and short and smiles when she sings and always wears short-sleeved dresses, even though it's the middle of winter, and the other is opposite in every way—tall and thin in a black dress with a high collar up around her long neck, stiff as a tree and a wrinkled old snarly face to match. Our two Baptist sisters are somewhere in between.

After the singing, my grandfather preaches a sermon, a short one, about Jesus being born, and then there's the Christmas play—every year, the kids in one of the classes get to put on the play of the birth of Jesus. It's called the Nativity.

One year my brother got to be Joseph. He wore his bathrobe over his clothes. The next year, I was a shepherd and wore his same bathrobe, because I didn't have one. One year, I got to stand at the pulpit and read the Christmas story from the Bible, because I was the best reader in our class.

Then presents. The kids in all the classes, and the grown-ups too, draw secret names of the people they're supposed to buy a present for. We all put our presents under the tree when we come in, so all of them, all the presents from everybody in the church, are piled all up, under and around the tree.

It takes a long time to hand them all out—they read out the name on the present, then one of the deacons brings it over to you—everybody in the whole church gets one. Sometimes you get a new baseball maybe, or a toy car, or a model tank or Army plane, but usually it's the 79¢ kind, the kind you just snap together without any glue.

Then, for last, every year my grandfather brings boxes of oranges and apples from the grocery, and the deacons give out an apple and an orange to everybody in the church. When I asked one year why he did that, my mother said it was because when my grandfather was growing up, people couldn't get fresh fruit all the time like we can, so it was a special treat to have an orange to eat, especially in the winter.

That's when my father told me that, when he was growing up, he got the same thing from Santa every year—a peppermint stick, an orange, and a new pair of overalls. It was a good year when he got the fancier kind of overalls, the kind with a zipper on the bib pocket instead of just a button—he said he walked treetop tall those years.

He also told about the year he and Uncle CC tried to stay up Christmas Eve and catch Santa, but he left their presents out on the front porch, instead of on the mantel over the fireplace, like every other year.

We are not out in the country at night very often, and I like the drive home after church, especially at Christmas, when it's always darker and more like nighttime than in summer, and sometimes there might even be snow.

I like to lay my head back on the seat as far as I can and look up through the back window at the sky and the stars. I like to turn and watch the cigarettes my mother or father toss out the window explode into little fireworks on the road behind us.

One night, coming home from Christmas service, we came around a bend in the road and saw, off across a field, a huge bonfire, leaping up in the sky, four or five men moving around it. The fire was taller than a house, the men looked like shadows lit up on one side but dark on the other.

My father told me they were probably clearing fencerows, that they burned the brush at night so they could see the fire better, see it and catch it easier if it spread to the grass, before it set a field on fire.

That spring, in English, I wrote a poem about it—

Fingertips of flame
reach

to bits of blaze
on black—

brush fire at night.

Glass Bottom Boats

My grandparents drove to Florida every summer for vacation. Daytona Beach.

My brother got to go a couple of times, then I was old enough to go once too. It was the summer before I started school.

The night before we left, I stood in the kitchen and cried and told my mother and father I didn't want to go without them. It was my first trip away from home.

They said they knew I would be o.k.

It was still night when we left, so we wouldn't have to stay at a hotel on the way. My brother and I brought blankets and pillows and made a bed and slept in the back of the station wagon where my grandfather usually kept his piano tools. When I woke up, we were driving around the side of a mountain in Tennessee.

When we got to Florida, we stopped at an old fort that had cannons, and that's where I saw the ocean.

When we got to Daytona Beach, we stayed in an old house with a sign on the porch post—

Kerwin's

Tourist Home.

It's where my grandparents stayed every year.

The room had two beds and a cot for my brother and me. If you had to go to the bathroom, it was down the hall, past other people's rooms, and sometimes you had to wait.

*   *   *

Every morning in Florida, we had breakfast at a lunch counter in a drugstore down the block from Kerwin's Tourist Home, except we ate in a booth and not at the counter. Also it wasn't lunch. It was the first time I ate waffles.

In the day, we went down to the beach and splashed around. My grandfather was teaching my brother how to swim, so I didn't get to go with them, far out in the deep water. I just stayed in the shallow part with my grandmother and dug around in the sand and picked up shells.

One day my grandmother was sick, so I stayed in the room with her while my grandfather and brother went out. There was a big storm that afternoon and the lights went off and my grandmother made up a game for us to play, where you toss coins at paper cups and you get different points for different coins.

Some days we went walking on the boardwalk, looking in stores. We watched them make taffy, and you could get a necklace made out of candy.

We went shopping for souvenirs, and I picked an idol head, carved out of wood, on a leather strap. But when we got out of the store, my grandmother read the label that said the idol head was carved to represent an ancient god, so she made me take it back and trade it. I don't remember what I picked next.

One day we drove to something called Silver Springs. They had alligators and a man who could milk a rattlesnake, which means squeeze the poison out of its mouth into a glass jar, but I didn't watch that. I stood by myself under some trees.

They also had boat rides. The boats had glass bottoms, so you could look down and see all the beautiful fish under the water as you passed over, but we didn't get to go on those.

The night before we left Florida, there were fireworks, and we went out and stood on the pier, crowded with people, and watched them—popping and banging out over us, and under us too, the colors splashing out, reflecting in the far, dark water.

*   *   *

One of the few things I have of my grandparents' is an old glass paperweight. I picked it off a pile of belongings waiting to be boxed up, when we were moving them out of their house.

It's a clear glass dome—you can look down into it and see a picture at the bottom, a color lithograph of a long, flat pleasure boat with a yellow canopy, passengers in hats and ties and dresses leaning over the low side, reaching down to the water, its green surface pocked in splashes of white, fancy writing scrolled around the picture's top edge—

Feeding Fish from Glass Bottom Boat
at Silver Springs
Ocala Florida.

Evansville

My father got a job driving a mail truck to Evansville, Indiana. That's when we moved out of my grandmother's house.

He got up at 4:30 six mornings a week, drove his two-ton truck to the post office and loaded it with bags of mail, then drove to Evansville, dropping bags off at little towns along the way. At Evansville, he loaded the truck up with more bags to drop off at the same little towns on his way back home.

My brother and I went with him some days in the summer. Since I wasn't in school yet, I got to go by myself other times too. Then, when I was in school, my father let me play hooky sometimes and go with him anyway.

On the days I went, I got up and dressed, then sat with him in the kitchen in the dark while he finished his coffee. Sometimes we split a cinnamon roll or I might eat a biscuit.

In the cool mornings, the truck smelled like old floorboard dirt, my father's heavy coat, his cigarettes and aftershave, the couple of greasy rags behind the seat with his toolbox.

The first stop, before the post office even, was the train depot, to pick up the bundles of newspapers left on the platform by the overnight train from Louisville. We dropped those off at the little towns too, along with the mail bags.

It was still dark after we loaded up and headed out of town, only a couple of other cars on the streets, empty sidewalks, just streetlamps shining circles of light down—then west out of town, out past West Side, into the country, trees and ponds and cows and corn, barns and tobacco, sometimes clouds of fog across the fields, lights in the farmhouses coming on.

I've had to look at the map to recall the route, but several of the stops I do remember—Gracey first, then Cadiz Cerulean Princeton Fredonia, then Crayne, where the post office was just a little store by the roadside, and two old men were always playing checkers on the front porch, except in winter, when they played inside—also where we got breakfast, my father a sandwich and coffee for his thermos, me an oatmeal pie and chocolate coke.

Then Marion, then Sullivan, then outside Sullivan we picked up the Dairy Dip lady, standing by the highway waiting for us, then riding to the next stop, Sturgis, holding her big purse and paper hat in her lap. The Dairy Dip was beside the road too, and we dropped her off before going on into town.

At Morganfield, the water in the water fountain smelled like sulfur and tasted awful. My father said it was because of the coal mines, by and around.

Outside Morganfield, we passed by the Army base where my father was stationed, where he learned sheet metal work. Part of the base was a prison camp for German soldiers captured during the war. They were allowed to paint pictures on the walls of some of the buildings. My father said you could still see the pictures on some of the barracks.

Somewhere along the way, we passed a sign, pointing down a side road, that said Cuba 6 Mexico 14. My father always said, "We're a long way from home now." I knew they were just the names of towns, still in Kentucky, but it did seem like a long way.

Neither town is big enough to show up on the maps I have.

Then Waverly and Corydon, where we picked up the old man who rode to the horse track on the other side of the river. He stood by the side of the road too, waiting for us, always in the same worn-out brown suit, hat and tie, like what I remember my great-grandfather wearing, except this old man's shoes were bright yellow, with tassels.

The old man spent most of the ride rolling cigarettes to put in the little tin box he kept in his coat pocket. Out of the corner of my eye, I watched his old hands with the white hairs sprouting out as he worked the papers and the tobacco pouch, watched him pull the drawstring with his teeth, crimping and folding, then licking the thin white stick between his lips. If it was winter, he held the little stick up to the heater vent to dry it out before putting it in his little box.

Sometimes I wondered how the old man got home at night. And the Dairy Dip lady.

At Evansville, we unloaded the last of our bags and loaded on the ones that were waiting on the dock for us. Then we had a break until the truck came in with the last of our load. We had hamburgers for lunch and sometimes napped on the pile of bags in the back of the truck while we waited.

At Evansville, I learned another of my father's nicknames. His name was Bernard, so he was Barnyard at several stops. At Cadiz, he was Muscles—thin and wiry, he didn't have many. At Marion, he was Mule Train, the operations code name for the ship he was stationed on in the Navy. At Evansville, the guys that loaded the trucks were Scotty and Big Bernie, so there my father was Little Bernie.

On the return trip, I didn't get out at as many stops, except always at Crayne, where we got ice cream that came in a cup with little wooden spoons—Meadow Maid Dairy, the label showed a cow wearing a straw hat. We always got chocolate.

In summer, if he wasn't running behind, my father would see wild asparagus by the road and pull over and pick some for us to snack on, or even enough to take home for supper. Once he pulled over to show me poke—we picked some of that too, to take home for supper, but only that once.

Back at Hopkinsville, we stopped again at the post office to unload before going home. In summer, it was still daylight, but in winter it was dark already and people were home for the night. Our house smelled like supper when we walked in, washed up and ate and told about our day.

I remember that one night after we got home, I was taking my bath and realized I smelled like my father—cigarette smoke, after shave, old worn canvas mail bags.

*   *   *

A couple of times my mother went too. I still got to sit by the window, though, because she always sat in the middle, by my father.

Once when she was with us, we stopped for a train at a railroad crossing somewhere out in the country. We were first in line, stopped right next to the tracks.

We were counting the cars clacking by, when a coal hopper went past with a man tucked up under the belly of it, a bundle under his head, sailing along on his metal bed just inches above the ground—flashing by then disappearing, on down the tracks.

After he'd rattled by and on out of sight, my father said, "Well, I guess that's one way to travel."

My mother said, "I just hope the poor man gets where he's going."

Nashville

Twice a year my grandfather drove to Nashville to buy Sunday School books and church supplies at the Southern Baptist Bookstore downtown. Sometimes we went with him, my grandmother, brother and me, sometimes my mother.

After the Bookstore we ate lunch at a cafeteria, where all the food came in little glass dishes they put on your tray. Even watermelon, chopped into little chunks, in a little glass dish.

The cafeteria was in a department store, where my mother and grandmother walked around and looked after lunch, while my brother and I rode the escalators up and down.

He had been to Nashville a couple of times before I was old enough to go. When he had tried to tell me about escalators, I somehow pictured them rising up the outside of the building—moving staircases rising up the side of the Life & Casualty Building, the tallest I knew of in Nashville, from pictures on t.v.

I was glad to learn the escalators were inside, and didn't go up that high after all.

*   *   *

We went to the car races in Nashville a couple of times. The track was next to an amusement park—the sign over the entrance had Humpty Dumpty wearing a crown, sitting on a rainbow, with the name—Fair Park—spelled out in lights.

At the races we sat in wooden bleachers under a roof, and watched the cars go around. I remember trying to read the billboards that lined the outside of the track. I don't remember seeing any crashes.

Once we bought souvenirs from a man walking around selling them from a tray. My brother got a Rebel soldier cap. I got a checkered flag I wasn't allowed to wave out the window on the trip home.

My mother told me they had once saved the money to take us to Fair Park without realizing until they got there that it was race day. Counting what they had, they figured we could go to the races, but wouldn't have enough money left for supper that night. So we went to the races, where they bought my brother and me hot dogs for supper, and they had popcorn.

Nashville was also where you went to visit people in one of the big hospitals, when they were very sick. We went there to see my grandmother a couple of times. Also my Aunt Kitten once.

A memory too early to be clear—we are driving to Nashville, and I am in the back seat with my great-grandfather. We had stopped at Stuckey's on the way, and he bought me a Popeye ColorForms set, and I am sitting next to him, playing with it. He is wearing an old brown wool suit, a tie, his hat on the shelf behind the back seat, thin yellow socks, brown shoes with little holes around the edges.

I realize now we must have been taking him to the hospital in Nashville for his last time.

The only other memory I have of him, he is at my grandparents' house, sitting in my grandfather's rocking chair, wearing the same wool suit, the same brown shoes, his hat on the table beside him.

*   *   *

Passenger trains were still running when my mother moved to Hopkinsville. Some Saturdays, my Aunt Kitten took my mother and grandmother and my mother's cousin on the train to Nashville for the afternoon matinee at the Opry.

After the show, there was always some time to kill before catching their train back. Sometimes they walked around the corner to Ernest Tubb's Record Shop to look at records, and my mother's cousin usually brought home one or two new ones—they had a record player at their house, which my mother did not.

Once, they thought they saw Cowboy Copas, in his rhinestone suit, duck into the back room of the store.

*   *   *

On one of his trips to the Bookstore in Nashville, I went with my grandfather by myself. We didn't talk much. He told a couple of stories. He ended one of them saying, "People are funnier than anybody," the first of many times I remember him saying it.

After the Bookstore and lunch at the cafeteria, my grandfather had two other errands. He'd had polio as a child, which left his legs different lengths, so he had to have his shoes made special. That day, we had to stop at the store that made his shoes for him. It was down a couple of blocks of run-down looking stores, a few buildings with neon signs and blacked out windows I knew would be bars.

Then, in another part of town full of old office buildings, we found a door on the sidewalk with a glass window, and painted on it—

Elmo Mercer

Music Publisher.

My grandfather had started writing songs, and Elmo Mercer was the man who was helping him.

The door opened onto a steep flight of creaky wooden stairs to another glass door with the same sign painted on it, which opened into a small room with a desk, a shabby couch and a piano.

I sat on the couch, while my grandfather and Elmo Mercer sat on the piano bench. My grandfather gave him some sheets of paper he had written on, then, as he sang the tunes, Elmo Mercer picked them out on the piano, and wrote the music notes on some other papers.

My grandfather published sheet music for a number of his songs. We even saw one of them for sale once on a rack at the Southern Baptist Bookstore.

All the music he published says the same thing—Words and music by Rev. Marvin Stinson, Arr. Elmo Mercer. For a long time, I thought an "Arr." was some kind of preacher, like a "Rev.," or something else in the church, at least maybe a deacon. But it only means he's the one that wrote the music notes on the paper.

*   *   *

One of my friends in high school decided finally to run away from home, to escape the father who beat him and the shit farm they lived on. He managed somehow to buy a Greyhound ticket to Nashville without his father finding out, skipped school one afternoon to get on the bus and go, but when he got there, he had no idea what to do.

100

He walked around the bus station and up and down the street a while, until a couple of old black guys noticed him, asked if he needed help, and took him home with them.

They fed him, let him sleep for the night on their couch, then called his father next morning to come get him.

★   ★   ★

I lived in Nashville a few months after college, but hadn't been back for many years until I returned to Hopkinsville once, to drive my mother and father down for one of her hospital appointments.

The appointment took much of the mid-day. My father and I killed time sitting around waiting rooms, walking corridors, then finding the cafeteria for lunch.

When we'd finished eating, we went out to a small plaza off the hospital cafeteria, where my father could smoke. There were benches, a small fountain, flowers.

Otherwise quiet, little to say as usual, in mid-smoke my father turned where he sat, to point to an upper floor of one of the older buildings rising behind us.

"That's the building my daddy died in," he said. "The eighth floor."

Over the course of my life with him, I recall my father saying hardly anything himself about his father's death—what I knew of it came from my mother and other family—it was something he never spoke of.

I could only respond with silence.

We sat quietly then—nothing else said for the few minutes more it took him to finish his cigarette, put it out—before going back inside to finish waiting.

Fair Week

Fair Week is always the second-to-last week before school starts, in August—it goes Fair Week, then the last week of vacation, then school.

Fair Week starts on Monday, but the Fairgrounds is just a few blocks away, on the other side of the river, so you can ride your bike over and watch them set up rides the Sunday before. Some of the trucks even get in on Saturday.

Every year my brother and I save our money over the summer to go a couple afternoons, collecting coke bottles or mowing yards. One year I made potholders out of yarn loops and sold them door-to-door. And there are always coupons in the newspaper you can cut out.

Then one night, usually Friday, we all go together, my mother and father and sister too.

Fair Week starts at noon sharp on Monday, when a paratrooper team from Fort Campbell does a jump, sky-diving into the Fairgrounds, into a big target in the infield of the racetrack.

We pick somebody's back yard to watch from, and put our money together to get something from Jarman's store to eat or drink while we're watching.

You sit or lie in the grass and watch the sky until you think you hear the plane engine churring somewhere, quiet, then louder, and there it is— the plane, circling over once, twice—then the bodies falling, specks you can barely make out, then the chutes popping open, one by one popping out and drifting down—two, three, six, more—and you can start to make them out now, men's bodies gliding down through the air then sinking finally behind treetops or rooflines and out of sight—us talking about what it would be like to be there and see them when they landed, see what it would look like when they hit the target, or where they would land and what would happen to them if they didn't.

★   ★   ★

From anywhere in West Side, you could see the tops of the Ferris Wheel and a couple of other rides up over the trees, you could hear the music and the people on the rides screaming and the barkers on loudspeakers and the big motors that run the rides. The breeze blew over the smell from the animals and the sawdust in the livestock barns, the smell of cotton candy and diesel.

At night, from anywhere, you could see the lit-up rides and the haze of light and dust yellowing up the summer sky over it all. And sometimes you even had a bedroom window you could see a little of it through. And you could lie in bed and listen to the noise of it, sometimes with the window open, go to sleep listening to the rides grinding, the riders howling, the barkers and game callers.

I described it once in a children's story I wrote, "Joyland"—it begins:

> We can see the lights
> of Joyland
> from our bedroom window.
>
> At night
> we lie awake
> and dream of it.
>
> Joyland
> is on the other side of the river
> that runs behind our house
>
> the lights like stars
> like constellations
> come swirling down to earth.

*   *   *

When it's just my brother and me, in the afternoon, we mostly just ride rides. Sometimes we play some of the games our father won't let us play when we all come together—tossing rings on milk bottles or popping balloons with darts or betting on the mouse wheel—because they're not as easy as they look, our father says, and they're all crooked anyway, even the mouse wheel, which I don't see how.

Every year my brother wanted me to go in one of the freak shows with him, and I never would, until one year some of his friends went with us, and we went in one of the spook houses and then one of the freak shows.

The spook house was House of Fear, and the sign was a big devil's head with horns and fire, and his open mouth was the door. But when you got in, you just wound around, back and forth through these narrow passageways with stupid mirrors and scary pictures on the walls.

I figured out later the whole thing was just the inside of an old tractor trailer with the big devil head hung on the side of it.

The freak show was Boneless Baby and London's Largest Sewer Rat, but it was so dark in there, and everything was in glass cases, so you could hardly make out what anything was, so you couldn't really tell if it was anything very creepy. The rat was dead anyway.

The night we all go together is usually Friday, right after my father gets home and cleans up—we get hot dogs at the Fair for supper. The lights are always brighter, but the Fair always seems noisier too, at night, and bigger somehow, and easier to get lost, even though it's the same size as in the daytime.

We always get to the rides last, never first. And it takes forever, every year.

We start in the big barns my brother and I never go in when it's just us, so my father can look at the animals and talk to the farmers about their pigs and goats and baby calves, and my mother can look at the cakes and pies, the quilts and needlework that won the ribbons. She says it gives her new ideas to try.

Then, we get our hot dogs and stand by the racetrack fence and watch the harness races while we eat. They're always on Friday, and my father likes to watch them, which is one of the reasons we go that night.

And they go on and on every year—the horses coming down the track so quiet the riders look like they're just gliding along on the air behind them, then closer and you can hear them and they pass by and you can see how hard the horses are working, their big muscles straining, how hard they're huffing, the drivers barking orders—then off down the track, gliding away into the quiet under the spotlights again, around and around, each time you think <u>has</u> to be the last one and hardly ever is.

Then, finally, rides. My brother and I ride all the usual ones together, and my mother rides the kids' rides with me, and even rides one or two of the big, upside-down rides with my brother. My father never rides, mostly stands and smokes a cigarette watching us.

One year one of the freak show tents had a wrestling bear that people could wrestle for money. When you walked by, you could hear the bear in there snuffling around. My father wanted to go in and see it, but my mother didn't like the idea.

And one year, there was a man who rode a motorcycle inside a big ball made of metal wire. We all went in to see that. People lined up around the sides of the wire ball, close enough to touch it. The man was already inside, on his motorcycle. He started riding it up around the sides of the metal ball, slower at first, then faster and faster, upside down, doing loops and figure eights, right in front of your face, looking like he was going to crash every time, and it got louder and louder and just too scary, so I had to go out and my mother came with me, so only my father and brother got to see all of that.

★   ★   ★

Saturday night is fireworks. We don't go to the Fair that night, my father says, because that's the night they let a lot of riffraff in—they want to make as much money as they can on the last night, so they drop the prices on everything, and that's when people without much money go.

But Saturday is fireworks. One of the streets to the Fairgrounds goes up a little hill, by some warehouses with a parking lot, and that's where we go for fireworks, two blocks from the Fairgrounds, with an open field between. The parking lot is not very big, so you have to get there early to find a spot.

Some people get out and sit on their cars or on the curb or stand around, but we don't get to. We sit in the car and wait, listening to the rides grinding around, somehow faster and louder on Saturday night, the music and the noise, the dust and smoke rising up in the yellow light over the Fairgrounds, getting yellower as the sky gets darker.

Then, above the noise, a crackle and muffle from the loudspeakers at the racetrack, some announcement to the people in the bleachers that means it's about to start, everybody in the parking lot shifting around, some standing up to see better.

Then, when dark finally comes, you hear it first—the fizz and whistle—
then see it, the first tail of smoke and sparks sizzling up into the night,
see, as I once put it in a poem—

>the sky
>at last
>bursting into wounds.

The Alhambra

Along one wall, a caravan moves majestically through the blue desert night, the laden camels, their impassive riders, across the dunes toward the lush but distant oasis, the stars clear and precise above the horizon.

On the opposite wall, the same caravan, moving across the same desert.

Above and around the proscenium and the screen, the towers of the desert fortress, the Legionnaires at their watch, their lamps at intervals across the battlements.

On the ceiling overhead, faint white clouds, like dreams—if you laid your head back on the seat and gazed up at them, they would begin to look as though they were gliding over, and you would begin to feel as though you were gliding too.

They used to have live shows there, but by the time I was growing up, it was only movies.

It was where my father saw Ernest Tubb in 1947, and where he took my mother to see Cowboy Copas and got mad and left her there because she wanted to stay afterwards to get Cowboy Copas's autograph.

It was where my mother and her mother went, along with half the town—it was so full, they said, that people were standing three and four deep all the way around the walls—all come to cheer along with the newsreel showing the war ending, showing the fathers coming home to their children, the sons to their fathers.

One of the Pentecostal churches uses it now. The marquee looks like a pegboard, all the bulb sockets empty. The side door opening onto the alley that used to be the Colored entrance is boarded up.

In the poster cases, two hand-painted signs announce a Prophecy Seminar. "Who Among You Will Witness The Last Days?" they say, above a picture of the world engulfed in flames.

Screaming Eagles

One Sunday afternoon, after Sunday dinner at my grandmother's, we drive my aunt to Fort Campbell so she can talk to a man behind a wire fence while we sit in the car and watch.

Sometimes we go to Fort Campbell after Sunday dinner, to watch the planes take off and land or just to drive around—my father helped build some new buildings down there when he worked at the sheet metal shop, so he knows his way.

The big sign at the gate says—

Welcome to Fort Campbell, Kentucky

Home of the

101st Airborne Division

"Screaming Eagles"

The guard at the gate has a white helmet and white belt and white gloves, and he always salutes when you drive through, even if you're not in the Army.

This time, though, we go to a part of the Fort I don't remember, and we sit in a parking lot, looking at some men penned up behind a high wire fence, walking around smoking cigarettes. My aunt is standing outside the fence, talking to one of them. She's beside some other women, some with kids, who are standing at the fence talking to some of the men too.

The fence is really two fences, with a gap between that's wide enough to keep people on the two sides from touching or handing things across to each other, even though a few kids poke their arms through the wire and try. Also, at the corner of the yard is another guard in a white helmet and white belt and white gloves, but this one has a rifle.

Years later, I will realize that was the stockade. That was visiting hour. That man my aunt was talking to would be my uncle.

And that's why she would wash her hair in the kitchen sink some Saturday nights after that and smell up the whole house.

And that's when she hung the Jesus cross on the wall above her bed. He didn't have any clothes on, except a blue sheet wrapped around his legs.

*   *   *

One Saturday afternoon, we are driving to Springfield, Tennessee, and the car is crammed full—all of us, plus my Uncle CC and Aunt M. My aunt and the man are following us in a different car. We're driving to Springfield, Tennessee so they can get married without having to wait as long as in Kentucky.

I have never been to a wedding. But it's a long trip.

Uncle CC married Aunt M. in Springfield, but that was twelve years ago, so when we get to town, we have to stop at a gas station and ask for directions to a man called Justice of the Peace. Then we get lost in some crumbled down streets along a river, with tumbled down houses propped up on stilts.

Then we find the right house and stop, and the wedding is this—my mother sits in the car with me and my brother, while everyone else goes in and gets married.

When they come out again, my aunt is still my aunt, but now the man is my uncle. Then they get in their car and drive off, and we all get back in our car for the long trip back home.

It's already night when we stop at a restaurant for supper. When the lady asks me what I want to eat, I say a baloney sandwich, and everybody laughs because they don't have baloney sandwiches at that kind of restaurant.

Then, I'm sitting in Uncle CC's lap in the back seat and the night is dark all around the car and all around us and he burns my arm with his cigar but it's an accident and he wets some tobacco in his mouth and puts it on the burn to take the sting out and it does but it smells bad and then I fall back asleep.

And that's all I remember.

*   *   *

In second grade, we started having Civil Defense drills. Every week, they brought all the grades to the gym for assembly and showed films about nuclear bombs and radiation and how some people were building fallout shelters and how much food and water to put in it and how you would use the toilet and how long it would be before it was safe to come out. Mrs. Turner even showed filmstrips about it in class.

And one day, we even got out of school at lunch, but we had to run home as fast as we could, and next day bring back a paper that marked down how long it took us to run home from school, in case we were attacked.

It was because the Russians might bomb us, and we needed to know what to do.

Some of the older kids said there was a secret underground bunker at Fort Campbell where they stored nuclear rockets and did secret experiments. Jerry Williams said his father worked on it when they were building it, and he was an electrician, and it was called The Birdcage, and it would be one of the first places the Russians would bomb probably, after New York and Washington, D.C., but his father was sworn to secrecy so couldn't tell about it.

I didn't know whether it was true, whether to believe it, but for the longest time, I would lie awake, afraid in the night, listening for the slightest odd or unusual anything that sounded like it might be an alarm or alert or even the bomb itself whistling over in the darkness, wondering if I would hear beforehand the churring of the plane that dropped it, the thud of it in that one second before we were all blasted away by a tidal wave of flames, like in the assembly films.

Most nights I would be comforted back to sleep by two sounds in the darkness I would later cherish, vivid in childhood memory—the grind of loaded semis, gearing their way up and over Belmont Hill, headed east out of town, or the screech and trundle of the freight trains, slowing on their way through town, even then already passing on through without stopping.

⋆　　⋆　　⋆

Part of Fort Campbell had been a prison camp for German soldiers captured during the war. The Army sent groups of them around to help farmers work their crops, since all the local boys had gone off to fight overseas.

My mother said her grandfather had a crew of them come help him harvest hay one summer, but they looked so miserable, and the thought of them being so far from home bothered him so much, that he only did it that one time.

★   ★   ★

For a while, my grandmother rented a room of her house to G.I.'s stationed at Fort Campbell—one of the rooms we lived in when we lived with her. They weren't building barracks fast enough for all the new recruits coming in, so people were renting out rooms of their houses for them to live in.

My uncle was a friend of one of the G.I.'s who lived at my grandmother's. My aunt met him at a wrestling match in the Armory, a big gym on the second floor of the Sheriff's Office and County Jail, next to the Alhambra Theatre.

My uncle had joined the Army to get out of trouble in Pittsburgh, where he grew up—just a street kid, he said. After he and my aunt met, he would get rides back and forth from the Fort to Hopkinsville, by waiting at one of those covered benches around town that said—Help Uncle Sam! Give a Service Man a Lift!—where people would pick soldiers up and give them rides to wherever they were going.

Or my aunt would sneak rides with some of her friends, down to Fort Campbell to meet him. My mother even drove her down once.

He was a jump instructor. He taught paratroopers how to jump out of airplanes, and how to land, like at Fair Week. He taught them how to do it without getting hurt, even when people were shooting at them.

★   ★   ★

Across the highway from the Fort Campbell gates is several miles of pawn shops and used furniture stores and laundromats and army surplus stores and restaurants. Some of the restaurants have signs with symbols for words. My father tells me the signs and the words are Korean, that they used to be Japanese. In a few years, they will be Vietnamese.

My father has brought my brother and me to Fort Campbell, to one of the pawn shops to buy a new record player. We get a new one, now that we've moved out of my grandmother's house.

The two big pawn shops in Fort Campbell are Hard-Hearted Hannah's and Soft-Hearted Sam's. You hear their ads on the radio all the time. We go to Sam's because we come to it first.

There are racks and racks of Army uniforms and guns in glass cases and rows of bicycles and t.v.'s and shelves of cameras and radios and record players. There is a real torpedo hanging from the ceiling, over the cash register.

My father gives me fifty cents to buy a 101st Airborne Screaming Eagles pin to put on my shirt pocket.

The record player we get has a handle, with speakers that swing out, so you can carry it around, and it plays the big records too, not just the little ones in the stacks that my mother keeps on top of the refrigerator and likes to play while she's cooking supper.

*   *   *

In town you'd hear them coming over but sometimes not be able to see them. But if you could see the sky or were out in the country, you'd see them practicing, flying in formation in and out of the big air base— strings of low-flying Hueys, popping the air like iron dragonflies, or full-bellied Chinooks, churning through the sky. You'd hear them at night too, practicing night runs, and the jets searing through the air, taking off and landing.

Sometimes they practiced bombing runs. They always announced it in the newspaper, so it wouldn't scare people. When my father would read to us about it, my mother always laughed because he pronounced "bomb" like "bum"—"They're dropping some bums at Fort Campbell this weekend," he'd read.

One year the story explained that they never use live explosives when they practice bombing runs. "All the bums they drop are dummies," my father read.

My friend lived on a farm in south county. He was walking one of their fields one night and, following the noise, came across a helicopter hovering over a beanfield with soldiers rappelling up and down, on ropes and ladders, practicing night drills.

He also told me that, hidden in the woods on one of their farms, was a log cabin his grandfather had built with his sons, when the sons were still young. It stood some forty years, until my friend's uncle went back once and found the yard trashed, the cabin burned, nearly to the ground.

They thought ever since that it must have been some Fort Campbell G.I.'s who'd spotted the cabin from the air during their helicopter runs—with no road or track to it, it was so well hidden that no one who hadn't hiked back to it would have had any other way of knowing it was there.

*　　*　　*

I thought it would be weird when my uncle came back from Vietnam, but it wasn't. We had watched the war every night on the news, watched them add up the numbers of the bodies, saw a lot of Screaming Eagles jumping out of helicopters into the jungle or the tall grass, or loading guys on stretchers, jumping back on.

We wondered if we would ever see my uncle on t.v., but also hoped we wouldn't. A couple of my friends also had uncles or brothers in the war, so they would be watching too.

He was gone four years, and I'm sure he was back home once or twice during that time, but I don't remember seeing him. When we found out he was coming home for good, we wondered if he might have been tortured or lost a leg or something. But he hadn't, and when he got home, it was only weird because he seemed bigger somehow, older, more like a grown man, like my father—when he left, he was more like a kid, like my brother.

Also, even though nobody told us, we never asked my uncle what he did in Vietnam. He never talked about it, and we just knew somehow not to ask.

After he'd been back a while, my uncle got a job at the factory where my aunt worked, one of the new little clothing factories that came into town after the big Elk Brand factory closed. He ran ten miles every morning before work, drank beer all day and much of every night and wrecked a lot of cars, thankfully without ever killing anyone, though spending some time in jail because of it.

He moved my aunt and my grandmother into a nicer, bigger house.

He sometimes took my brother and me for drives in the country after Sunday dinner. He liked to go down to south county, which is flat, with long stretches of straight two-lane, the back roads into Fort Campbell, where we'd go to get a part for his car, or to stop in one of the pawn shops, or just to get milkshakes.

The first time I rode in a car going a hundred miles an hour was in the back seat of a red Mustang convertible he had for a while—a car he flipped into a ditch just a couple months later—no seat belt, Motown blasting out the radio into the wind blasting into my face, more afraid than I had ever before been in my life, too afraid, for many reasons, to ask him please to slow down.

When I mentioned to my mother how fast he drove, she made us stop going with him.

He taught me how to strike a paper match one-handed, without tearing the match out of the book. He showed me a game of chicken they played in the Army—blindfold a person, give them a lit cigarette, have them twirl it in their fingers a few times then stick one of the ends in their mouth, hoping it's the right end.

If our phone rang at odd hours in the night, we knew it would be my uncle—when he got into trouble, most times he called my mother first to help him out, before he called my aunt. And she always did. And they had many long talks at our kitchen table in the late hours.

One night, several years after I'd moved out but still lived in Hopkinsville, my uncle called my mother at three in the morning and asked her to please send my father to come pick him up, and to get there quick, he was in a craps game at somebody's house on the other side of town, the buddy he came with had gone and left him there, he didn't know where, and he'd won a lot of people's money that he wasn't sure they were going to let him leave with, so could my father please come get him quick as he could—and he told her the street and house number.

But my mother thought that part of town was too rough to send my father, so she called me to go pick him up instead. I finally found my way through a part of town I'd never been in before, didn't know was there even, streets running under a Parkway overpass, ending at a gravel road that a shot-up sign said led to the county dump.

I picked my way through a few streets of trashed houses, no streetlights or signs, slowed down along what I thought would be the right block but didn't see him, and couldn't, until he stepped out of the shadows between a couple of houses, flicking his lighter to show me it was him.

One night my aunt tracked him down in a trailer park outside Fort Campbell, found him at another craps game, chased him and a few others out of the trailer with her pistol and took a couple shots at him as he ran across a field and into some trees.

He said later the only thing that saved him that night was the evasive maneuvers he'd learned in combat training, and I don't think he was joking.

After I finished school, my uncle got me a job at the factory where he and my aunt still worked. He was warehouse foreman. I loaded coveralls into boxes and the boxes onto shelves.

We sometimes went for beer after work—he knew every cinder-block-and-blacked-out-windows beer joint in town, and out. But even though he asked many times, I never would go out with him at night—just too damn dangerous.

He said to me once, over a pitcher after work at the pizza place down the street from the factory, as seriously as I ever saw him, that he thought the Lord must have some purpose in mind for his life. He'd spent four years in Vietnam being shot at by people he couldn't even see, thought more than once over there about shooting himself, lost a lot of buddies, then come home only to have his own wife take a few potshots at him too, wreck more cars than he could remember—the Lord doesn't let you survive all that, he said, without having some purpose in mind for your life, some mission.

He said he just couldn't figure out yet what the mission was.

*   *   *

Part of Fort Campbell is in Tennessee, where the drinking age was lower than in Kentucky, so that's where my friends and I went, to the bars and clubs and the couple of strip joints between Fort Campbell and Clarksville, the next big town on the Tennessee side.

There was a beer joint in Clarksville with a blue electric guitar mounted on the wall behind the bar. The guy who owned the place said it had belonged to Hendrix, whose band played there sometimes when he was stationed at Fort Campbell. The guy said Hendrix had given him that guitar after he'd discharged and moved to Nashville, before going back to Seattle. Nobody knew whether to believe the guy.

More often, we drove across the state line to buy what we needed and brought it back to drink, usually at Iron Bridge or one of the other spots we knew along the south county backroads, or somewhere on my friend's farm.

Sometimes we'd stop at the drive-in theatre just back on the Kentucky side of the line, old and shabby and run down, but staying in business by showing porn on weekend nights to Fort Campbell G.I.'s and south county farm boys. The Family Drive-In, it was still called.

We'd go there to drink, and sometimes bum pot off people, if we passed by a car and smelled it.

The G.I.'s were usually pretty good, sometimes roll you a joint, or at least share a roach. They'd talk to you, tell you where they were from, where they'd been or were going.

*   *   *

There was trouble after the trailer park incident. The judge told my aunt and uncle that the best thing would be for him to just leave town for a while, until it all blew over. My uncle had an Army buddy in Houston with a construction business, so he moved down there and worked construction a while, waiting to see if anything would happen.

My aunt stayed behind, and wouldn't have gone with him even if she could.

I drove them down to Nashville to put him on the plane to Houston. At the airport, we drank and shot pool in the VA lounge while we waited.

On the way down, my aunt had me take a different road out of Fort Campbell, toward Nashville, a route I didn't know. A few miles on the other side of town, the highway passed by an old roadside motel, still in business but seedy and run down now.

As we passed by it, my aunt told me that was the motel they had spent their honeymoon in.

The sign by the road was in the shape of a huge heart, two stories tall, arrow piercing through it, neon once lighting the banner unscrolled across it, with the name—Purple Heart Motel.

My aunt, beside me in the passenger seat, watching it go by, said, to no one in particular, "Purple heart motel…."

From the back seat, my uncle—"That was a hard time, wasn't it sweetheart?"

My aunt—"Shut up, Elroy," the middle name he hated, and hated even more to hear her use.

*   *   *

I was in high school when the U.S. and North Vietnam agreed to release all their P.O.W.'s, a first real sign the nightmare war I was growing up with—and could barely remember a time before—might somehow actually come to an end, the world somehow finally, impossibly changed.

I was at a basketball game, at the high school gym. I had left a few minutes before the game ended to beat the crowd, was standing by the street, waiting in the January cold for my brother to come pick me up, when I heard the noise from the gym behind me suddenly quieten, the game whistled to a stop, a muffled voice announcing something on the P.A., then a roar, a roar of people bursting louder, more unburdened than for any game.

The first few people trickling out then—what happened, what was …

P.O.W.'s

                                    the war

        Vietnamese

             all the prisoners

free   coming home   free   free

    home

                        the P.O.W's free

           all the P.O.W.'s

all the prisoners now

                    they're all of them
                          coming home

Iron Bridge

The river runs by the L&N tracks, coming into town from the north, swerves at the cemetery to cut West Side off from downtown, passing first behind the Little River Motel, which used to mark the outskirts of town on US 41, the old Dixie Bee Line; passing under the North Main bridge, along by the seed company silos, around Todd's brickyard, coming into West Side under First Street bridge, where the banks flatten, with a scattering on both sides of tumbledown shacks among the brush and kudzu, where a few black people still lived; passing into downtown behind the courthouse and the block-long building with the Sheriff's Office and County Jail, the Armory and the Alhambra Theatre, along by the low brick garage that was my father's sheet metal shop, and across the street from it the homesite of the town's first settler, and on the opposite bank the row of brick-front sheds where my grandfather had his shoe repair shop; passing on under Seventh Street bridge, along the stretch of gone Illinois Central warehouses and on through downtown under Ninth Street bridge—a park promenade now, but then—thick brush and weeds on both banks overgrowing the dumped junk, old tires and appliances, a couple of rusted car bodies visible under the muddy water, rising to the surface in dry summers; passing on, swerving west again and south to skirt the back of West Side Park and opposite, on a steep rise, the town's first graveyard, Pioneer Cemetery, that once would have overlooked the first homestakes of the village of Elizabeth, as it was then named; passing on beyond the lumberyard and then on out of town, bending around the back lot of the Fairgrounds, out into farmland, tracing through south county before hooking sharp west again, stretching finally to empty, a county over, in what once was the Cumberland River but is now the eastern shore of an Army Corps of Engineers lake.

*　　*　　*

When we walked or rode our bikes downtown we didn't like going by First Street bridge. There weren't many houses along that last street by the river, and they were all as broke down as the handful of shacks scattered out along the banks. When you crossed the bridge, you saw people down there, fishing sometimes or cooking outside or sitting in chairs.

Nobody ever said anything to us, but we didn't like the way they looked at us when we crossed over.

Running alongside the Ninth Street bridge was a huge water pipe, painted black, connecting West Side to downtown. Some of the older kids would try to walk across it. There weren't any handholds, so you had to walk it like a tightrope. It would have been a bad fall.

Once, we drove over the bridge and looked down and saw a kid sitting on the big pipe, straddling it, scooting across on his butt.

If you jumped the outfield fence at West Side Park, there was a path down to the river, down through the weeds and underbrush, opening out onto a mud flat at the water's edge. We went there to shoot BB guns mostly, mostly at whatever river trash you could always find along the bank.

Once, we tried to see how far we could follow the river out of town from West Side Park. We made it quite a way, scrabbled through brush and over rocks, on beyond the backyards of the last few houses of West Side and out the edge of town.

Just past the lumberyard, though, we came to a rock ledge jutting out of the bank that made a little cave, with a pile of blankets and bags and cans, that looked like somebody was living there. We didn't see anybody, though, so we got scared and turned around and went back.

*　　　*　　　*

After Evansville, my father got a route closer to home, carrying mail from Hopkinsville to the little towns west, in Trigg County and down by the Lakes. People he got to know told him about places along the river to fish, or let us drive across their farms to get to places, so that was mostly where we went then.

My Uncle CC took me fishing a couple of times to places along the river he knew, a couple of old mill sites in south county. We went on Sunday afternoons, after Sunday dinner at my grandmother's, in whatever battered old car he was driving at the time, every one of them sagging on the driver's side under his three-hundred-pound weight, smelling like the cigar stub he always kept in the corner of his mouth, sometimes lit to smoke, sometimes just there to chew.

These were the only times I spent alone with Uncle CC, neither of us talking much, both quiet by nature. It was time he spent, anyway, mostly untangling my line or cutting it loose from a snag in the water or out from the underbrush where I had cast it again by accident.

Uncle CC was a kind and patient man. But he only took me fishing that couple of times. I don't remember ever catching anything.

★   ★   ★

A high school friend was from south county, where his family owned several farms. He took me to Iron Bridge, a rusting old trestle over the river, on a gravel lane connecting two county backroads.

At one point, the lane passed through a quarter-mile grove of walnut trees planted evenly along both sides, a drive once leading to some farmstead or house long sunk into the landscape, now, of plowed fields and scattered woods.

The deck of Iron Bridge was loose planks that clattered and thumped, and the old metal groaned when you drove across.

Kids came out there, mostly to drink or pop off pistols. Under the bridge, a broad stone ledge jutted out into the water, but to get there you had to pick your way down through the brush and the weeds and the junk that had been dumped down the bank, a couple of old car bodies half buried in the mud shallows at the bottom. Most people stayed up on the bridge or along the top of the bank or up by the roadside.

My friend and I decided once to see how far we could follow the river, walking the bank south from Iron Bridge. We went in February, when there would be fewer snakes.

There were stretches of mud flat or rock ledge we could walk over, stretches of brush and vines to hack through, sometimes places we'd have to climb to the top of the bank to find a way by.

We'd gone much of the afternoon, had already considered turning back, when we came around a bend and saw downriver, high on a mud bank, the ground eroding away beneath it, an old plank cabin, collapsing into weeds, long abandoned, no sign of road or path leading to it.

We agreed that was something to see, but having seen it, we didn't need to go there, so turned to retrack our way back before the light faded, still not getting back to Iron Bridge and the car until after dark.

Years later, I wrote some lines from that afternoon. They ended up in a poem called "February"—

> The copperhead and moccasin
> are sleeping
> vein deep in the blood of winter.

I sent my friend the book with the poem. He said he liked the book. The one passage he picked out and said he liked in particular, though, was those three lines.

I hadn't told him, and haven't, that they came from that afternoon we walked the river.

⋆   ⋆   ⋆

A few yards south of Iron Bridge is a weed-and-gravel drive leading off the road, curving up a rise, disappearing behind the trees to end at an old white frame church house, set on piled stones at the corners for a foundation, a crude handmade cross on the steeple and an open shed for an outdoor meeting place in back. The sign nailed on the wall says Spring Hill Baptist Church.

The drive is cabled off at the road to keep cars out, but people go up there anyway—you find bottles and cans and trash.

The church looks like it might still be used, somehow, by somebody, though not often. The building is old, but still kept up. The front door is padlocked. Looking in the windows, you can see the pews and other furniture are disarranged, with a little trash scattered around, but there's no vandalism, nothing torn up.

Late one night, my friend and I were at Iron Bridge, drinking, and decided to walk up to Spring Hill Church. There were no other cars around, so no one else would be up there. We took what beers we had, and I took a screwdriver from out of the glove compartment—I wanted in the church that night.

It was August, and a clear night, the mudfrogs, katydids and nightjars filling it. The church is tucked in a clearing in the trees at the top of the rise. That night, the grass of the lot was tall but not overgrown—it had been cut sometime that summer. A broken window in back had been patched over with cardboard.

My friend resisted, but I waved him off and unscrewed the padlocked hasp from the door. The hinges were loose, so the door scraped the floor when we forced it open and stepped through, into the church vestibule.

Inside was cool, smelling of old, worn and varnished wood, with clear enough moonlight through the few windows.

We stayed just inside the door, went no further, only enough to see and to remark on things we could see better now than through the windows—the crude pulpit, the hand-hewn cross on the wall behind. We speculated on who could still be using the church and how often, how long it had been here, the wonder it hadn't been ransacked.

We only stayed the few minutes, marked the moment before leaving by singing, in best form, a verse and chorus of "Diamonds in the Rough," our harmonies on the hymn rich and redolent of the cool dark wood of the old sanctuary.

Leaving, we closed the door without my bothering to reattach the lock, then walked back down to Iron Bridge for the drive home.

*   *   *

There was a small table in the vestibule of the Spring Hill Church, just inside the door.

We left two empty beer cans on it that night, my friend and I—a shame I have not reported or recorded until now.

Tiny Town

My mother was fifty-eight when she met the twin sister she didn't know she had.

My grandfather called her one afternoon and told her someone was at their house who wanted to meet her. My grandparents brought the sister over, and they met, for the first time they remembered anyway, in my parents' living room.

The sister had spent some twenty years trying to track down their family. She had found, still living, their father, two older sisters, and two of their father's brothers. My mother was the last to be found.

And, for whatever reason, my grandparents never would tell her, so my mother first learned her real name that day—Florine. Florine Flowers.

They, the twins, were born in Burkesville, Kentucky, east of Bowling Green, the youngest of four, all daughters. Shortly after they were born, their father went north to look for work enough to feed them all. A few months after he'd gone, their mother left the two older sisters with her family in Burkesville, took the twins to the Willowdale Orphans Home in Bowling Green and wasn't seen or heard from again.

The one twin had been adopted out before the orphanage closed, before my mother was sent out on the orphan train, and she had grown up, and still lived, not far from where they had been born.

Eventually, their father moved with the two older sisters to Indiana, where they all still lived, close by each other. One of his brothers still lived in Burkesville, but the other lived in Tennessee, east of Nashville, some hundred miles from Hopkinsville.

A reunion at the Tennessee uncle's was planned for a couple months later, in October, when all the family could be there, all but the older uncle, who didn't travel—a trip to visit him in Burkesville was planned for after the holidays.

⋆   ⋆   ⋆

I came back for the reunion, a Sunday in October. In the days before, my mother didn't talk much about it, mostly just to say how unbelievable it all was, how she never could have guessed she still had family or guessed they had been looking for her all these years.

She said once she just felt like somebody had brought something back to her that she didn't know she'd lost.

She did say she was nervous about it, worried what kind of people they would be, whether we'd all like each other and get along or not. She said once that she worried they might want something from her, or need something, and she had no earthly idea what she would do if they did.

We left mid-morning Sunday for the two-hour drive, my father insisting on driving and insisting we all go together. So instead of taking my car, the four of us snugged into his truck—my father and me, my sister and mother between. My brother and his family, my grandparents with them, drove down separately.

The morning was crisp, blue and clear, a cloud or two drifting, the trees and fields beginning to color into fall. The best route, by luck, kept us off the Interstates, mostly following a couple of the old federal highways into and through Nashville.

The directions were clear and easy enough, on beyond Nashville, through pasture land and woods, a small town or two, then the last little town, a scattering of houses and farmsteads—then a mailbox number—the white frame house, a few pieces of farm equipment by an open tractor shed, the long gravel drive—

—several other cars already there, my brother's among them, pulled in and about, the driveway running along the broad front yard, past a line of sugar maples, ending at a great pin oak shading the side porch of the house—the clutch of people gathered there shifting, turning, watching us pull in and park.

My mother's sister comes over from the group, stands waiting, my mother squeezing my hand as she gets out of the truck—

"Did everybody make it?" she says.

"Everybody's here," says her sister, "all waiting to meet you."

She takes my mother's hand, leads her over to where the circle of people has opened around an older man, standing in the shade of the pin oak—he is round and ruddy-faced, full white hair, muscled and raw-boned in a western shirt, cuffed jeans and work boots, his name embossed in the hand-tooled leather belt with silver buckle.

He has worked as a heavy equipment operator all his life, and still does—though, at age eighty-two, not as much in recent years.

He stands awkwardly, stooped forward, thumbs in his belt loops.

Her sister leads my mother over to him.

"Daddy," she says, "this is Florine."

The old man, tears on his face, does not move.

"Can you forgive me?" he says, barely whispering.

My mother steps up, they hug.

"It's all right," she says, patting his back.

Then, leaning back in his arm, to look up into his face—"It's all right," she says, "I know you did the best you could."

She told me later she had wondered all her life what she would say to him if she ever got the chance, and didn't know then what she would say, until that moment. But as soon as she said it, she realized she had known it all her life to be true.

★   ★   ★

Her sister introduced my mother then to the rest of her family, standing by their father—their two sisters, both widowed, one there with a daughter; their Uncle Roy and Aunt Golda, with two of their children and several grandchildren.

They had set up tables, spread them in the tractor shed, Roy and Golda had bought chicken, people brought covered dishes, pies, jugs of tea and soda. We ate Sunday dinner from paper plates, visiting and talking in pairs and groups around the porch and yard, before all gathering together into the house.

That afternoon, my mother's sister told what she had gone through to track the family down, how she started out trying to find their mother, and had found one of their mother's sisters, but the sister said she didn't know anything and didn't want to talk to her anyway, so that was a dead end, and that's when she started looking for their father.

Their father said, for his part, he never heard from their mother again either, after she left, and he hadn't cared to go looking for her. She might have gone back to West Virginia, where she had some people.

Uncle Roy told how, after their father came back to Burkesville and found out what happened, the two of them did everything they could to try to track the twins down. How they went to every orphanage and county office they could find in that end of Kentucky and Tennessee, how, later, they drove by schoolyards in different towns too, and watched for the school children, thinking or hoping the twins might still be somewhere close by and would be easy to recognize if they were still together.

My grandfather told how the church he was pastoring at the time was one of the churches providing for the children when the orphan train brought them to town. My grandmother told how that was the way they came to meet my mother the first time, among the cribs set up in the parlor of one of the big houses along the main street of Elkton.

My mother's father said he was just glad to know she had ended up in a good home.

By chance, Uncle Roy had worked most of his life as a contract mail carrier, like my father, mostly driving routes out of Nashville, up into Bowling Green and eastern Kentucky. He told how he had an overnight route for several years that brought him through Franklin, Kentucky, in the early morning, how for a couple of those years he stopped every weekday outside Franklin to pick up a teenage girl, who rode with him for the twelve miles to her factory job the next town over.

After my mother's sister tracked Uncle Roy down, and they started comparing stories, they realized that she had been that teenage girl—that for nearly two years, the niece he and his brother had spent so many years looking for had been riding in the truck with him every workday morning that whole time.

The rest of the afternoon passed, again, with people clustering in groups and pairs, my mother and her sisters and father talking a long time together, my father and Uncle Roy talking the mail business.

Aunt Golda drove my niece over to look at the home of a country music star who lived close by, driving her right up to the gate to look in, my niece said. My brother was impressed to learn from one of Roy and Golda's daughters that our family was descended from a branch of Robert E. Lee's family—impressed until some weeks later, when my father said to him that half the people south of the Mason-Dixon Line, black and white alike, could claim blood kin to Robert E. Lee, and most would be right to do so.

By late afternoon, my father was ready to leave, wanting to get back to Hopkinsville before dark, my mother's father and older sisters ready too, with a long drive ahead of them, back to Indiana. Plans were made for a second reunion in Burkesville in the spring, where my mother would meet her other uncle, and she and her twin made plans to visit each other over the holidays.

We parted and left then, the day still clear and blue as grace, though with the October light softening, shadows lengthening toward evening. For the drive back, I was snugged into the middle with my sister—my mother wanted to sit by the door so she could roll down the window and smoke on the way home.

*   *   *

I didn't come back for the Burkesville reunion, or for the two trips to Indiana my mother made to visit her father in the next couple years, before he died. Since Roy and Golda lived nearest, and my mother said she enjoyed their company the most anyway, she and my father made a number of visits back to their house over the next few years.

They planned several of their visits to Roy and Golda's for times I would be back in Hopkinsville, so I could drive them down. We usually spent a Sunday afternoon with them, Uncle Roy telling more about the family, my mother and Aunt Golda talking children and needlework and church, my father and Roy talking trucks and mail hauling and farming, which Roy still did a bit, on the few acres they had.

Aunt Golda always made a pot roast she knew I liked. And she always made a point to find a minute to talk to me about her concern that I wasn't married.

⋆   ⋆   ⋆

Between Hopkinsville and Nashville, just north of the Tennessee line, is a crossroad spot, Tiny Town, Kentucky, where two of the old federal highways cross. It was a tourist stop at one time, one of the last ones before Nashville on the road coming down from the north.

I have an old picture postcard of Tiny Town. It shows a motel, a Gulf gas station, Davis Snack Shop. The back of the card reads—

Tiny Town, Ky.
One Stop Tourist Accommodations
24 Hour Service
Air-Conditioned Motel
SUPER SERVICE STATION
Air-Conditioned Restaurant

There's a convenience store at the intersection now, a bar-b-que place that's sometimes open, a couple of roadside cigarette stands—Kentucky taxes are lower, so people come up from Tennessee to buy them—a few crumbling buildings, overgrown outbuildings.

Passing through Tiny Town, on the way back from the first reunion, I had a few shots left to finish off a roll of film, so took a few last pictures through the truck window, as we pulled into a stop at the four-way—blurred images of that day I have now, of the old Tiny Town Motor Lodge sign, still standing by the road, the once neon arrow now pointing across a field of cornstubble to a ruined barn—pictures of newer signs, for Tiny Town Trailer Park, Tiny Town Baptist Church.

As we pulled through the intersection, my mother, looking out the window said, to no one in particular, "Old Tiny Town."

A silence, then my father—"It is somewhat smaller than most, isn't it?"—the last said as we drove the final miles home, flametips of the sumac along the roadside and fencerows flaring up, lighting the way, the sky's last silver closing the October Sunday into dusk.

Benny

My grandfather used to fix shoes. He had a shoe repair shop in a little yellow building by the river. It was between a used furniture store and a barred-up, empty garage.

We would stop by to see him whenever we went downtown.

I liked going there. I liked the smell of the leather and the shoe polish and the machine oil. I liked the sound of the old machines, chugging and clattering, the belts slapping on the wheels and pulleys. I liked to bounce up and down on the old chrome chairs in the window.

And I liked to visit Benny.

Benny was a guy that worked for my grandfather sometimes. Benny couldn't hear. He had two hearing aids with wires running down into the little boxes in his shirt pockets. But they didn't seem to help much.

Benny couldn't talk very well, either. He could make noises, but they weren't words, so mostly he made a kind of sign language that you had to try to figure out.

I was scared of Benny at first. But he would always give me a piece of gum or a sour ball when we stopped in. And sometimes, when it was just me by myself, Benny would get me a free coke from the cooler in the corner.

He had this quarter with a hole in it on the end of a wire. He could push the quarter into the slot, let me get a pop, then pull the quarter back out.

He would only do it when my grandfather wasn't looking. Then he would wink at me and laugh and make a sign for me to not tell.

So, after a while, Benny and me became friends.

We would see Benny other places around town too, mowing somebody's yard or picking up pop bottles along the road, or just walking somewhere.

Some Saturday afternoons, Benny was an usher at the Alhambra Theatre. He got to wear a red coat. He took the tickets at the door, and then he walked up and down the aisles with a flashlight to make sure nobody had their feet up on the seat in front of them.

Every time we saw Benny out somewhere, we made sure he saw us. We would wave and he would always wave back.

I used to stay at my grandparents' house during the day, when my mother and father were at work. A lot of times there was nobody around for me to play with.

But sometimes, when there was nothing for Benny to do at the shoe shop, my grandfather would send him over to do some job around their house—pulling weeds around the porch or painting the tool shed or burning some trash in the alley. Then, when he was finished, Benny would play with me.

Benny helped me build dirt forts for my army men. When it rained, he showed me how to make matchstick boats to float in the gutter stream that ran down the street along the sidewalk.

When I was playing with Benny, though, I had to watch out for some of the big kids. The big kids were o.k., most of the time. But sometimes they were mean. They were especially mean to Benny.

They would call Benny bad names and yell stuff at him. Then they would laugh about it because they knew he couldn't hear them. Or they would act like they were making sign language to him, but it wouldn't really mean anything, and they would laugh at him when he tried to figure it out.

Benny acted like he didn't know they were being mean to him, but I think he knew. When he saw them laughing, he would just laugh too, even though they were laughing at him.

Sometimes the big kids would make fun of me too, when they saw me playing with Benny. Or if they were being mean to Benny, and I wouldn't do it with them, then they would start being mean to me too.

I wanted the big kids to like me, but I was afraid of them. So, if Benny and me were playing, and some of them came around, I would usually tell Benny good-bye and go in the house.

One afternoon, some of the big kids were playing baseball at the schoolyard. Usually, they wouldn't let me play with them, because they said I was too little. But this time they were letting me. I had even gotten a base hit once, and our team was winning.

Benny came walking along and stopped and watched us for a while. The big kids were too busy with the game to pay much attention to him.

Then, late in the game, between innings, Benny motioned me over to him and led me to where our bikes were parked. He stood beside my bike, held the handlebar, and started making signs to ask me if he could ride it.

I didn't know what to tell him. Benny had never asked to ride my bike before. I didn't even know he could ride one. And my mother and father had told me not to let anyone else ride my bike, because one time I let Terry Winders borrow it and he wrecked it and bent the back wheel up.

Before I could figure out what to do, Jerry Williams came over and started shouting, "Hey! He's trying to steal your bike!" All the other kids came around then.

Larry Ezell called Benny a bad name. And Frankie Wright pulled up a handful of grass, snuck up behind Benny, and dumped it on his head. It made Benny jump, and everybody started laughing at him. Then Benny started laughing too.

But then Robbie Morris started yelling, "Get your hands off his bike!" and swatted at Benny's hand with a bat. Some of the other kids started yelling, "Yeah! Quit trying to steal our bikes!"

I still didn't know what to do. I wanted to tell them to stop it, to leave Benny alone. I wanted to tell them that Benny was my friend, and that I hated it when they were mean to him. But I couldn't.

Instead, all I could say was, "I think he just wants to ride it some."

Then Jerry Williams shoved me and said, "No he doesn't. He's trying to steal it, and you're too chicken to stop him."

And Frankie Wright shoved me toward Benny and said, "Yeah, make him stop," and he called me a bad name. Some of the other kids started yelling at me to stop him too.

Then Benny made a sign toward my bike again. I still didn't know what to tell him. But finally I shook my head that it was o.k.

Benny swung his leg over the seat, pushed through everybody and took off.

I thought he was just going to ride up and down the street, but he rode off across the school yard and up Second Street. He turned back to wave, then disappeared around the corner onto Fowler, headed toward downtown.

By this time, all the other kids were laughing and making fun of me and saying I'd never see my bike again.

When I wouldn't say anything back to them, Robbie Morris said, "What's the matter? Forget how to talk?" He started calling me Benny Junior and asking me if I'd forgotten how to hear too.

Then they all started picking up their gloves to finish the game. But Jerry Williams said he didn't want any chickens on his team, and he wouldn't let me play anymore.

So I went and sat against the corner of the school building and watched them and waited for Benny to come back. I was wishing he would come back soon, because I was worried about my bike. But then I was wishing he wouldn't, because I knew everybody would just start making fun of me again when he did.

So I just sat and waited.

Finally, the game was over, and everybody started gathering up their stuff to go. Jerry Williams stopped in front of me and said, "Guess you'll be walking from now on."

And Robbie Morris said, "Or maybe you can fly, like a chicken," and everybody started laughing at me again.

They all got on their bikes and rode away. A couple of them called back, "See you later, Benny Junior," and a couple of them made chicken noises, and then they were all gone.

I just kept sitting there and sitting there. It kept getting later and later.

I knew it was way past supper time, and I was going to be in trouble, but I couldn't go home without my bike. And I didn't know where Benny was or when he would be back.

Finally, when it was starting to get dark and the streetlamps were just starting to flicker on, Benny came riding back around the corner, back down Second Street, and across the school yard to where I was sitting.

He stopped in front of me, got off my bike and held it out for me. He was smiling, like always. But as big as I've ever seen.

I didn't know how to ask him where he'd been or why he'd been gone so long. I just took my bike back, and Benny made a sign for "Thank you."

Then he took one of my hands, turned it palm up and put something in it. It was a ring from the big gumball machine at Cayce's Hardware, downtown.

The ring looked like a gold crown, with green plastic emeralds.

Benny turned and walked away, off across the school yard, looking back to wave good-bye again, before he disappeared up Second.

I put the gumball ring in my pocket. Then I rode home as fast as I could, trying to think what I would tell my mother and father about why I had missed supper.

Saturday Night

On Saturday nights, my mother and father would get things ready for church the next morning, polishing shoes or sewing or ironing shirts. My brother would study his Sunday School lesson.

I would go over to my grandmother's side of the house, to watch wrestling with her and my aunt.

To get there, I would have to go through the room where my great-grandmother was, which was also my grandmother's room. My great-grandmother was in her nineties and crazy, and I was afraid of her, even though mostly she just slept.

The room was always dark and hot. Except in the hottest part of the summer, there was always a small heap of fire in the coal grate, and still my great-grandmother lay under quilts in the big iron-frame bed, which she also shared with my grandmother.

Some of the quilts she had made herself, some forty or fifty or even sixty years before, and my grandmother was always making new ones with scraps of material she brought home from Elk Brand, where she and my aunt worked.

It smelled like old hair in there, and like the coal-oil lamps on the mantle. You couldn't turn on the electric light in her room, because it scared my great-grandmother for some reason, and she would start crying, or really just whimpering, because no tears would come out.

When the lamps were lit, shadows pooled up in the corners of the room and the ceiling, and the light flickered and waved, like the darkness was pushing against it, trying to take over again.

I was afraid of her, but sometimes, when I knew she was asleep and knew that no one else would come into the room, I would go over to her bed and look at her.

Only her head, or maybe an arm, would be out from under the quilts. She was nothing but bones, with wrinkled skin stretched over them.

One of her strokes had left her right eye so it could not close, and sometimes I would lean over and look down into it—dark and bottomless and open forever—trying to see what it was seeing.

The t.v. was in my aunt's room. The three of us would sit together on the couch that folded out into my aunt's bed. Wrestling was on for a whole hour.

My grandmother's favorites were Jackie Fargo and Len Rossi. She didn't like Sal Weincroft, and she especially didn't like the Bass Brothers, because they wore diamond tie pins and diamond rings and were always hitting at the good guys with their pearl-handled walking sticks.

Sometimes my aunt would have a coke, and the three of us would split it.

When wrestling was over, I would tell my aunt and my grandmother good night and go back through my great-grandmother's room to our side of the house.

My mother and father would already be in bed—a big fold-out, metal bed in the kitchen that they kept behind the door during the day.

In the winter, they would set it up where my father could reach up over his head to the gas burners on the stove and turn one on in the night if it got cold, and turn it off again when it got hot, because there weren't any coal grates on our side of the house.

If it was very cold, my brother and I would sleep with them. We would lie in bed, the four of us together, listening to the Opry on the black plastic radio that sat on the counter by the sink where my father could reach it too.

So Saturday night would end—my aunt's t.v. mumbling in the next room, my great-grandmother sailing around in her lost world, and me trying to stay awake long enough to hear Hank Snow sign off his part of the show, long enough to hear him say—Good night. Good luck. Good health. And may the good Lord always be proud of you.

Sunrise Service

Some things happen in life that sound made up when you tell them—the moment is somehow too composed, too coincidental, the poignancy too convenient. So, with the last time I saw my mother.

I had come to Hopkinsville the week before her birthday, in November. She was bedridden by then, but still at home at my sister's house, and in good spirits. We'd had a good visit.

I left early Sunday, as usual, for the long day's drive ahead. That morning I'd gotten away early enough, before dawn, to take a favorite route out of town, through south county, twenty or so miles to the Interstate, a narrow two-lane winding through farmland and forest patches, the road I would have taken to my friend's farm—a slow drive at best, the back roads and creek crossings, the mud ponds and ruined barns, a life's landmarks unrecognizable as such to others, but familiar and memory-worn to me.

The drive had gotten even more slow in recent years, as south county had become home to a growing Mennonite community—a number of families moving down from Indiana and Ohio mostly, buying and re-cultivating the land from the many farms, like my friend's, that had gone under during one or another farm crisis some thirty, forty years before. Their black, horse-drawn buggies had become a familiar sight in town, as well as on the county's roads, and so were a familiar caution.

That morning, the fields had settled into the first real cold of winter, thin frost dusting the soybean- and corn-stubble, rimming the pond edges, spreads of low fog here and there over the sinks and shallows, the narrow road weaving, but roughly following along the river south and west, dawn beginning to gray the sky, kitchen lights coming on in the houses along the road and scattered among the trees.

Coming into a wide, blind curve, I know, by the droppings in the road, to slow and watch for them, and coming out of the bend, I see them in the lane ahead of me, a quarter mile down a long, straight stretch, a line of black buggies—three, four, no, the full length of them coming into view—six black buggies, all clopping steadily, patiently along, as if in procession.

I slow, keep distance, unsafe to pass, which I wouldn't do anyway, for fear of spooking the horses. From that far back, I can still see their white breath huffing into the chill air, can see the black hats and bonnets, the blankets about the shoulders of the little families bundled in the seats under the buggy canopies.

Then, off to the right, a low rise, a hill, and coming into view, a wood-frame church house, a gravel lane up to it, and there—another line of them, two, three more black buggies, rolling in a line up the lane, a scattering of others already parked in the churchyard, blankets on the horses, one or two with feedbags—an elder couple scuttering in the church house door, opened, shut quickly against the cold.

And so I follow, and at such distance.

One by one they turn, then, the line of black buggies in front of me, off the hard road, up the gravel lane to the church house—the first, then a second following, the line slowing as the horses make the corner—a third, then the next and the next—one by one, the line of them re-forming now, rolling up the low ridge—and then the last, six black carriages in all, horses steaming in the November dawn—to church, to sunrise service, the black procession of them passing, one by one, stately as death, steadfast, eternal as life.

Sunday Morning

Before the names were changed to numbers, it was called The Dixie Bee Line. And they used to say it was a mighty good road, if you were looking for a road for leaving—north to Evansville and Terre Haute and Chicago, south to Nashville and Chattanooga and Atlanta.

It's one of the roads I take out of town, returning from my visits to Hopkinsville. Just north of Kelly Station, in the early light of Sunday morning, a faded billboard, collapsing into a cornfield, shrinks away in my rearview mirror. It shows a giant honey bee, black-and-yellow striped, smiling and waving a white-gloved hand.

Follow Dixie Bee—it says—Hopkinsville 27, Nashville 98.

I am awake these mornings earlier than I should be, with a full day of driving ahead. But I get up as soon as I hear my father making coffee. It will be a while yet before my mother is up, and this is one of the few hours I have to spend alone with him. He knows this, and I think he looks forward to it and would be disappointed if I didn't get up to visit with him, though, of course, he would never say so.

We sit in the kitchen talking, half-dressed, watching night begin to thin away to first light beyond the peach trees in the yard.

He asks about work and tells me about some job he knows of and thinks I could get if I wanted to think about coming back home.

He asks about the route I will take on the drive back, asks if it will take me through Virginia. It always does, and I tell him so. He asks if I will go through Bristol or Richmond or Roanoke, and I never do, and I tell him so.

He talks about things he's heard on the news, asks me what I know about them, asks if I know where places like Jordan or Bosnia are, if they're anywhere near Greece or Italy—places he knows from when he was in the Navy.

By dawn, I've gathered my things into the car, my mother is up, making a lunch for me to take. I call my brother once more. He's dressing, going over his morning's sermon. I tell him to come visit sometime. He says he should, though in fifteen years he never has, and likely never will. He tells me I ought to get home more often. I tell him yes, I should.

Then, without waiting for breakfast, I tell my mother and father good-bye. As I pull away from the house, they are standing inside the screen door, my mother waving, my father holding their little dog in his arms so it won't make a break for the street.

Out of Thornton Gap, I take the ramp onto the Parkway, October morning opening out clear and crisp.

It comes to me that this year, for his birthday, I will give my father an Atlas of the World. With an Atlas of the World, he would be able to find any place he heard about. He would be able to see where I live now, the route I take to get there. With the whole world opened out on his lap before him, maybe distances would not seem so great.

The Parkway takes me east, then north, through Muhlenberg. I dial through the church services on the radio, looking for gospel or bluegrass. At the Central City exit, I pull into the first toll booth, as a quartet is beginning "Let the Lower Lights Be Burning."

The woman in the booth is middle-aged, with graying hair, in a blue uniform.

"Morning," she says. "Getting off here?" she asks.

Off to my right, on a low ridge, thick smoke hovers and clings around a small barn, where tobacco is being fired. A man in a heavy coat with a hunched gait is walking up a dirt path toward it.

I hand the woman my money.

"No, ma'am," I say. "Passing through."

ACKNOWLEDGMENTS

An earlier version of "Seining" appeared in *Fourth Genre*.

"Hobo Signs" and "Sunday Morning" appeared previously in *Good River Review*.

"The Alhambra" appeared previously in *Timbuktu*.

With gratitude to—

CW, TN, HF, JB, GRH, DG / RB—friends, fellow pilgrims all

KS—for seeing the poetry in Hopkinsville

ABOUT THE AUTHOR

Tony Crunk is a native of Hopkinsville, Kentucky. His first collection of poetry, *Living in the Resurrection*, was the 1994 selection in the Yale Series of Younger Poets. He has published several subsequent collections, including *Biblia Pauperum* (Accents Publishing), as well as a number of works in other genres, including fiction, drama, and children's books. He lives in St. Louis.

www.ingramcontent.com/pod-product-compliance
Lightning Source LLC
Chambersburg PA
CBHW021639120626
46545CB00002B/615